Target Your Life

A GUIDE TO GET YOU FROM WHERE YOU ARE TO WHERE YOU WANT TO BE

Target Your Life

A GUIDE TO GET YOU FROM WHERE YOU ARE TO WHERE YOU WANT TO BE

By L. A. Tobleman

Copyright © 2024 by L. A. Tobleman

All rights reserved. No portion of this book may be reproduced in any form without written permission from the author, except as permitted by U.S. copyright law. Contact: l@lifeinelements.com for permissions.

First Edition: April 2024

ISBN (paperback): 979-8-9896905-1-0
ISBN (e-book): 979-8-9896905-0-3

www.lifeinelements.com

This publication is designed to share the ideas and experiences of the author. It is sold with the understanding that the author is not rendering professional advice. The advice and strategies contained herein may not be suitable for your situation. You should consult with a professional when appropriate. The reader's use of any suggestions, recommendations, or ideas in this book is at the reader's own discretion and risk. The author shall not be liable for any loss or damages, including but not limited to special, incidental, consequential, personal, or other damages, caused by following any of the suggestions, recommendations, or ideas in this book.

To Luke, my greatest blessing, may your life be
filled with joy as you fulfill your callings and dreams.

CONTENTS

INTRODUCTION……………………..…….……….9

SPIRIT……………………………………..……………11

HEALTH……………………….…..…….………...25

PRESENTATION…………….……..……...………43

JOY…………………………………..……………..57

ORGANIZATION………………..…..……...……77

YOUR FUTURE…………………………..……91

CONCLUSION…………………..…………….125

ACKNOWLEDGEMENTS………...……...………..127

INTRODUCTION

In my early twenties, I was attending college in a town I didn't like, working toward a degree that wasn't my passion, and engaged to someone I didn't want to marry. I was living my life like a leaf in the wind, going where I was carried by a force that wasn't my own. One day I was reading the novel *Ellen Foster* by Kaye Gibbons and was inspired by the main character, Ellen. She stated that lack of planning had been a mistake and that she was going to take control and decide how her life would be. That declaration struck a chord in me. In short, I took a good look at my life, broke my life into different parts or elements, and figured out what I wanted in each element. This book will guide you through the process I implemented and help you examine elements of your life, figure out what you want in each (your targets), and take aim at the targets you set for yourself through actions. You have the power to design your life, but you must know what you want and be willing to work for it.

Below are the different elements on which we will focus. We'll start with spirit and build upon each to help get you to the self and life you desire. All of these elements make up a whole and are intertwined, but to get very clear about what you want, we're going to pull them apart and zoom in on each separately.

As I take you through the process, keep in mind that your effort and dedication will dictate your results. I recommend working on each element for at least a month. If you try everything at once, it will become overwhelming. Focusing on each element for the suggested duration gives you time to clarify what you want and allows your thoughts, actions, and habits to become established.

No matter your age or circumstances, you have the power to change and direct your life. It's never too late to get yourself on track and point your life in the direction you want it to go, but as far as I know, we only get one life. My wish is for you to make it count and head in the direction you want now. Let's begin and get you where you want to be!

SPIRIT

In this book spirit will encompass presence, gratitude, giving, and spirituality. I've found that if this element is ignored, it's hard to get the rest to work. If this element is tended to, it gives you a foundation for the other five elements. It is something that can't be taken away from you. You can be in peak health and suddenly get sick or injured. You can have the perfect job and lose it. You can be in a relationship with someone you love, and he or she can end it. However, the practices and habits you build in the element of spirit are always there and serve as a base on which you can always rely.

To begin each element, there is an exercise to examine it in your current life. Take a few minutes and list ways you feel you're off track in the element of spirit in one or two words.

Now, take a sticky note or another piece of paper, write the opposite of each word, and post that positive list over the negative. For example, if you wrote distracted, replace it with present. This will give you direction in creating the target you want to aim for. It also will be a good barometer for how close or far off you are from where you'd like to be. We are all in different places. You know you and know where you're on target and where you're off target. With each element, give yourself more time where you require it.

Presence

Presence is simply being with, accepting, and experiencing the moment you are in, not living in the past, resisting what is, or fretting about the future. Being in the present moment is important to remember throughout this book and your life. You have your goals, dreams, and desires, but it's important to enjoy the now along the way to your targets. Don't wait to enjoy your life. Each moment, is all that there is. Aspire to be with, sense, and experience each moment in the way you want to experience your life. All these moments add up to the life you live. At the same time, remember to go easy on yourself. It's impossible to be 100 percent present or anything else 100 percent of the time. With each element, know your target but give yourself some slack. Just because you get off track doesn't mean you've failed. Think of yourself as an arrow moving toward your target. You may get blown off course a bit, but you have the power to aim at the target again and again. Take set backs as an opportunity to learn and course correct.

Let's talk about some strategies to work on being present. First, take some time and find a peaceful image to place in the space below that makes you think of being present. To give you an idea, I found a photo of a butterfly drinking nectar from a flower. This will be an image you can picture when you need to come back to the now.

My presence image:

At the end of each chapter, there will be a four week calendar to schedule actions for each element. The first will be to picture your presence image three times - once in the morning when you wake up, once in the afternoon, and once before you go to bed. While you're picturing the image, take three very slow, deep breaths. Inhale filling up your lungs all the way down to your belly, hold, and exhale slowly and completely. This will help you return to the now throughout each day.

For the second strategy, I want you to pick a practice that strengthens your ability to be present. Some examples are meditation, yoga, petting your dog, listening to beautiful music, or walking in nature. Pick one activity you can commit to doing each day. Pick something you will enjoy, an amount of time, and a time of day you feel will work with your schedule. This can always be changed as you and your life evolve. You may pick meditation for five minutes to start, but as your schedule changes or you find you really enjoy it, you may change the time to twenty minutes. There may be times you find yourself very busy and need to decrease the time. The key is to keep it simple and not make it feel like a chore. Just enjoy doing it with the intention of being present. Write down what you'd like to try, and at the end of this chapter, you'll add it to the calendar along with your presence image and breathing.

*My presence activity:*_____

*Time:*_____

If you find yourself gripped by your past, it's important to address that. Struggling to make peace with and accept the past can rob you of living your life now. Picturing your presence image while deep breathing and your presence activity can help take your focus off the past, but sometimes it's very difficult to let go without help. I would recommend talking with someone such as a counselor or psychiatrist if needed.

Gratitude

Nothing can shift your life quite like gratitude. Being in a state of thanks changes your whole outlook on life. In each moment look for the good in the situation. To help you focus on being in a state of gratitude, either at the beginning or at the end of each day, write down five things you're grateful for. Many have recommended this, and there is a reason why. It will get you in the habit of looking for and keeping your focus on good things throughout the day. Find a notepad, a journal, or a device to write five things you're grateful for each day. This is something you will add to the calendar at the end of the chapter as well.

*My gratitude journal time:*_____

Your life may not be anything like what you want right now, but focusing on what's wrong probably will only make you miserable. Find the good where you are now, even as you strive to make changes and improve your life. This is so important. Life will have ups and downs and will never be perfect. When you're feeling off, down, or things are tough, stop and find something to be grateful for. Keep your focus on gratitude. Being able to find what's good and give thanks for it will give you the mindset to keep your aim.

Also, be sure to express gratitude. Consistently tell those in your life, such as your family, friends, and coworkers, thank you and what you appreciate about them. Tell the person who bags your groceries thank you. When someone does something kind for you, write a thank you note or call and express your gratitude. Let people doing various jobs know how much you appreciate their hard work. You get the idea… spread gratitude!

Giving

Another act that can shift your life is giving. Giving will have such a positive impact on you and our world. We all have a different amount of time we can offer, different talents and skills, and different passions and heartstrings. Pick one thing you care about such as animals, the homeless, children, the elderly, or the environment. Now pick an amount of time you can commit to giving each month. Maybe it's one day per month. Maybe it's once a week. Now do an internet search or call an organization and find a volunteer opportunity for an area you care about. If you're not sure where to start, try https://www.volunteermatch.org. Sign up to volunteer for something you feel is a good fit for you. Again, this will be added to the calendar at the end of the chapter.

*Giving activity:*_____

*Time:*_____

Something fun to do in the area of giving is a random act of kindness. It can be as simple as smiling and saying a friendly hello to a stranger. You can put a pretty potted plant on a coworker's desk. You can buy the coffee for the person behind you in line. You can help someone carry something heavy to their car. If a friend isn't feeling well, offer to bring them some groceries or make them some soup. It doesn't have to be big or cost anything. Try it out! It's fun! Make it less than random and start a habit by scheduling one time to do a random act of kindness each month, and you may just want to keep adding more.

*Random act of kindness ideas:*_____
_____
_____
_____

Also, throughout your day shift your perspective as you go about your daily obligations. Think of each act as an opportunity to give. If you're studying for an exam, think of the act as giving yourself knowledge you'll use in your life or career. If you're taking a difficult college course, think of the act as giving yourself a credit for your degree. If you're comforting your infant in the middle of the night, think of the act as giving your child love and security. If you're making food for your family, think of the act as giving your family nutrition. If you're cleaning, think of the act as giving yourself and others a comfortable, sanitary home. You will tend to these tasks either way, but if you do them with the mindset of giving, you'll be giving to yourself. At the same time, don't let this turn into saying yes when you don't want to or can't. You have to set boundaries. Don't overextend yourself. If you have too much on your plate, ask for help and give yourself permission to say no.

Spirituality

Spirituality is very personal. Some have this down. Some may feel lost or confused in this area. I am not here to tell you what to believe. What I will say is that being connected to something bigger than yourself gives you strength and direction. I will also say it's important to have a strong footing in what is right and wrong for you. When you compromise your standards, you loose a bit of respect for yourself. For example, I've always had a deep passion for protecting the environment. When I was about thirteen, I had a crush on a boy. One day I was hanging out with him, and he threw some trash on the ground. To me this was a horrible act, but I ignored it, said nothing, and didn't even pick it up myself. Trying to fit in with him, I shut down a part of myself. That was a long time ago and just a silly childhood event, but I still remember how bad I felt when I compromised my values.

Since this is such a personal area, I'm going to be less specific about what you should do. You may already belong to or want to join a specific religion or find a connection to a higher power through the wonder of nature. Find what resonates with you and write down what you'd like to do for your spiritual practice. Maybe it's going once a week to a place of worship or going on a hike in nature. Maybe it's reading something uplifting and inspirational or listening to or watching something through technology. Maybe it's taking time to pray each day. Decide what works for you and write it down to schedule it in your calendar at the end of this chapter.

*My spirituality practice:*_____

*Time/place:*_____

The next thing I want you to do for spirituality is get clear about your rights vs. wrongs. This doesn't have to be a long list. Always being kind or treating others the way you want to be treated covers a lot. The important thing is to know this for yourself and stick to your values. Now, at the same time, all humans mess up. We can never be perfect. Forgiveness of yourself and others is crucial. In fact, I would recommend reflecting on what you need to forgive yourself and others for monthly. Take the blunders as lessons. Learn from them, let them go, and continue on aiming for your standards. Take some time and answer the following questions.

What are my rights vs. wrongs?

What do I need to forgive myself for?

Who do I need to forgive?

If you find it difficult to forgive, I'll share a practice that has helped me. First, find a time when you can be alone and let all your feelings out in writing. This not a time hold back, but don't linger and wallow for too long here. The end objective is to release and move on. Once you've expressed your feelings, try to see things from the other person's perspective (or yours at the time if you're forgiving yourself). This is not to excuse the wrong, but sometimes it can help to understand how or why the wrong occurred. There are, of course, times when there is no explanation to be found. Next, see what lessons there are to be learned, and, if appropriate, tell the person you forgive them. Finally, accept what happened, shred your writing, and let go.

Spirit Target

Now it's time to get clear about where you want to be in the first element. Review your list at the beginning of this chapter and any thoughts that have come up as you've read. Take some time to reflect and then set your spirit target below. As you form your target, be very specific about what you're aiming for. The more specific you are, the easier it will be to figure out how to get there.

◎

With your target set, it's now time to create a plan to reach it. Knowing what you're aiming for is really the first step. Once you have a clear picture of what you want, you can think about what it will take to attain it. I suggest breaking your plan into simple steps that will build upon each other until you realize your desire. An exact path of steps might not come to you all at once. That's okay. Come up with one or two to begin. After you accomplish the first step or two, decide on the next step and keep going in that manner. Some of the practices suggested in the chapter might even be steps if you're not sure where to begin. Use the space below to brainstorm ideas, and then the following chart can be used to list out steps toward your target. You may not need all the spaces or you may need more. Just keep going until you hit your target. If needed, the chart can be found on my website at https://lifeinelements.com/downloads/.

Target Your Life

20

Taking Aim with Actions

Here's where you are going to pull back the bow and set your arrow off to where you want to go. You can't get anywhere just thinking about it. You must have a plan and take actions. In the following calendar, take the steps you chose earlier in this chapter and fill them in. Again, visit my website at https://lifeinelements.com/downloads/ where you can print the calendars for each chapter if you're reading this as an e-book or would like to work on an element for more than four weeks. Each day check them off as you do them. The goal is to make these actions become habits in your life. I also want you to schedule at least one step toward your target in the calendar as well. At the end of the month, you will pick the next step to keep on the path to your target. Taking small steps toward your target is what will get you there. To help encourage you, at the end of each week give yourself a little reward if you've completed all your actions. It can be something as simple as giving yourself time in the day to read a book with your favorite tea. You could pick up a bouquet of flowers from the grocery or buy yourself a shirt you've been eyeing. Just something quick and simple to motivate you. You'll continue this process as you move through the book building on each element.

Schedule in…	Pick at least 1 step toward your spirit target & schedule…
<ul><li>Your giving activity</li><li>Your random act of kindness</li><li>Your spiritual practice</li><li>Your forgiveness check (Do you need to forgive yourself or anyone else?)</li></ul>	Spirit:_____

Spirit

	Sunday	Monday	Tuesday	Wednesday	Thursday	Friday	Saturday	Reward
Week 1	__ AM, Noon, & PM: Close your eyes, picture presence image, and take 3 slow, deep breaths __ Presence activity __ Gratitude journal	__ AM, Noon, & PM: Close your eyes, picture presence image, and take 3 slow, deep breaths __ Presence activity __ Gratitude journal	__ AM, Noon, & PM: Close your eyes, picture presence image, and take 3 slow, deep breaths __ Presence activity __ Gratitude journal	__ AM, Noon, & PM: Close your eyes, picture presence image, and take 3 slow, deep breaths __ Presence activity __ Gratitude journal	__ AM, Noon, & PM: Close your eyes, picture presence image, and take 3 slow, deep breaths __ Presence activity __ Gratitude journal	__ AM, Noon, & PM: Close your eyes, picture presence image, and take 3 slow, deep breaths __ Presence activity __ Gratitude journal	__ AM, Noon, & PM: Close your eyes, picture presence image, and take 3 slow, deep breaths __ Presence activity __ Gratitude journal	
Week 2	__ AM, Noon, & PM: Close your eyes, picture presence image, and take 3 slow, deep breaths __ Presence activity __ Gratitude journal	__ AM, Noon, & PM: Close your eyes, picture presence image, and take 3 slow, deep breaths __ Presence activity __ Gratitude journal	__ AM, Noon, & PM: Close your eyes, picture presence image, and take 3 slow, deep breaths __ Presence activity __ Gratitude journal	__ AM, Noon, & PM: Close your eyes, picture presence image, and take 3 slow, deep breaths __ Presence activity __ Gratitude journal	__ AM, Noon, & PM: Close your eyes, picture presence image, and take 3 slow, deep breaths __ Presence activity __ Gratitude journal	__ AM, Noon, & PM: Close your eyes, picture presence image, and take 3 slow, deep breaths __ Presence activity __ Gratitude journal	__ AM, Noon, & PM: Close your eyes, picture presence image, and take 3 slow, deep breaths __ Presence activity __ Gratitude journal	

Daily Spirit Reminders…

- Focus on the positive
- Express gratitude
- Shift your perspective on obligations as an opportunity to give

Spirit

	Sunday	Monday	Tuesday	Wednesday	Thursday	Friday	Saturday	*Reward*
Week 3	__ AM, Noon, & PM: Close your eyes, picture presence image, and take 3 slow, deep breaths __ Presence activity __ Gratitude journal	__ AM, Noon, & PM: Close your eyes, picture presence image, and take 3 slow, deep breaths __ Presence activity __ Gratitude journal	__ AM, Noon, & PM: Close your eyes, picture presence image, and take 3 slow, deep breaths __ Presence activity __ Gratitude journal	__ AM, Noon, & PM: Close your eyes, picture presence image, and take 3 slow, deep breaths __ Presence activity __ Gratitude journal	__ AM, Noon, & PM: Close your eyes, picture presence image, and take 3 slow, deep breaths __ Presence activity __ Gratitude journal	__ AM, Noon, & PM: Close your eyes, picture presence image, and take 3 slow, deep breaths __ Presence activity __ Gratitude journal	__ AM, Noon, & PM: Close your eyes, picture presence image, and take 3 slow, deep breaths __ Presence activity __ Gratitude journal	
Week 4	__ AM, Noon, & PM: Close your eyes, picture presence image, and take 3 slow, deep breaths __ Presence activity __ Gratitude journal	__ AM, Noon, & PM: Close your eyes, picture presence image, and take 3 slow, deep breaths __ Presence activity __ Gratitude journal	__ AM, Noon, & PM: Close your eyes, picture presence image, and take 3 slow, deep breaths __ Presence activity __ Gratitude journal	__ AM, Noon, & PM: Close your eyes, picture presence image, and take 3 slow, deep breaths __ Presence activity __ Gratitude journal	__ AM, Noon, & PM: Close your eyes, picture presence image, and take 3 slow, deep breaths __ Presence activity __ Gratitude journal	__ AM, Noon, & PM: Close your eyes, picture presence image, and take 3 slow, deep breaths __ Presence activity __ Gratitude journal	__ AM, Noon, & PM: Close your eyes, picture presence image, and take 3 slow, deep breaths __ Presence activity __ Gratitude journal	

HEALTH

On to the element of health. This may be my favorite element because you have so much power to influence your health and how you feel through lifestyle choices. The state of your health has such a profound effect. If you don't feel well, it's harder to enjoy your life. Each person's body is very unique with different needs that change throughout life, so for the element of health I'm going to give you some general and basic ideas and principles. Also, I'm not a doctor, and this chapter is not to be taken as medical advice. Now, let's talk about impacting your health in a positive direction.

In this chapter we're going to look at sleep, exercise, nutrition, stress reduction, and any "hang-ups" you may have to get your health on track. Again, everyone is at a different place in their life. You may have nine hours of uninterrupted sleep every night, compete in Ironman Triathlons, and meditate an hour a day, or maybe you're struggling to get five hours of sleep, eat fast food for most meals, and feel you have no time for exercise. Wherever you find yourself is all right. You have to begin where you are. So, take a moment and list where you feel you are off track in the area of health below. Then, just like in the first chapter, write the opposite of each word and post that positive list over the negative. For example, replace sluggish with energetic or weak with strong.

Sleep

Ah, sleep! Sleep is so crucial, but somehow in our society it's sacrificed too often. I've found you have to protect and fight for your sleep.

We will begin with how much sleep you need. It would be lovely if we could all just wake up naturally (maybe that's something you want to aim for in your life), but for now I'll assume you have some schedules and obligations that, to some extent, dictate when you have to wake up. In general, adults are advised to get around eight hours of sleep. Some people need a little less, some a little more. To find out how much you need, find a time when you're not overly tired and you have a few days you can wake up naturally. Note what time you go to bed and wake up. This will give you an idea of how much sleep you need. Write this down.

I need _____ hours of sleep.

If you have to wake up at a certain time, count back how many hours of sleep you need and give yourself a time to aim to go to bed. I'd recommend giving yourself fifteen minutes extra to actually fall asleep.

My bedtime:_____

Okay, now you know how many hours of sleep you need with a general time to aim to get in bed. Try to be somewhat regular with the time you go to bed and wake up. It helps to have a consistent sleep schedule, but don't feel like you've failed if it doesn't happen every night. Allow yourself to have fun if there's a late event. Just come back to that targeted bedtime the next evening.

Here's a list of ideas for enhancing your sleep and making sleep something to enjoy and look forward to. Try some out and do what works for you.

* Lower the lights in the evening. Keep bright overhead lights off and use soft lamps.
* Stop screens at least an hour before bed.
* Read a good book to relax you into sleep.
* Keep your bedroom organized, clean, and clutter free.
* Create a beautiful and relaxing bedroom. Find a picture from a decorating magazine or website you love and recreate it. Furniture is expensive. If your budget doesn't allow for new furniture right now, get some accessories or try antique shops, garage sales, and used furniture stores. A little TLC, paint, new fabric, and imagination can go a long way.
* Treat yourself to luxurious sheets. Try silk or bamboo.
* Find some comfy blankets.
* Check your pillows and mattress. Is it time for replacements?
* Treat yourself to some comfortable or beautiful pajamas.
* Make your room as dark as possible. Do you need light blocking window treatments? Is there an electronic device shining light all through the night that needs to be unplugged, covered up, or moved?
* Do a sound check. Does street noise or a snoring partner disturb your sleep? Get noise reducing drapes and/or a sound machine.
* Keep the temperature cool.
* Add a potted plant or a few.
* Try eating a few hours before bed. I was surprised by how much better I sleep when my body isn't in full digestion mode.

* Alcohol also affects how well you sleep. If you have a drink every night, try a night without it and see if you sleep better. You may find you want to give yourself some nights off.
* Cut caffeine out in the afternoon and evening.
* If you worry or have a racing mind at night, try journaling your thoughts before you go to sleep.
* Drink a calming tea like chamomile in the evening. I would advise not to drink too much right before you go to sleep or you may wake up in the middle of the night needing to use the restroom.
* Create a relaxing evening routine.

Exercise

Our bodies are made to move. Exercise is essential for health. Your body needs it. It promotes good circulation, increases nourishing blood and oxygen to your skin, allows your skin to release excess salts and wastes, gives you a healthy glow, slows the aging process, increases resistance to health problems, is good for your mood… I could go on and on.

If you've already got this piece to the health puzzle down, fantastic. Keep it up! If you don't, that's fantastic too because your life will be changed by beginning it. You don't have to run marathons. You just have to move your body.

Exercise is something you want to evaluate and set goals for often. Let's take a look and see where you find yourself on the exercise spectrum. Start by visualizing what being fit means to you. Take some time and think about how you want exercise to benefit you. Do you want to feel strong, fast, and flexible? Do you want your clothes to fit better or not get winded walking up stairs?

Write your thoughts down…

_____
_____
_____
_____
_____
_____
_____
_____
_____
_____
_____
_____
_____
_____
_____
_____
_____
_____

To me being physically fit comes from three areas: cardio, strength training, and stretching/flexibility. What I've found to be essential is finding a way to incorporate these three areas in a way I enjoy and works for me. If you pick activities you don't like at times and places you don't like, you're probably not going to keep them up.

First, I want you to think about the time of day you want to devote to exercising. For me, if I don't do my exercises in the morning, obligations throughout the day crowd out my exercise. For someone else, exercising after a day of work may be the perfect way to decompress. Perhaps you have little kids you're looking after, and their afternoon nap time is great for you. As you pick this time, keep in mind it doesn't have to be set in stone. It's important to be flexible, not just in the limber sense. Things happen that throw you off schedule. Life changes, and you can change your time. I just want you to think about what will work best for you generally.

*My best exercise time:*_____

Now, I want you to think about where you'd like to exercise. Personally, I love working out at home. I don't have to worry about getting dressed up or take the extra time driving somewhere. For some people the act of going to a workout facility or club keeps them motivated. Some might want to get outside in a park. What would you like best?

*My best exercise spot:*_____

Next, think about whether you like to exercise solo or with others. Do you like time by yourself? How about having your dog as a walking or running partner? Would you be more motivated with a friend or friends as workout buddies? Does the idea of a large group class or a sports team sound good? How about having a personal trainer?

*Who I would like to exercise with:*_____

If you already incorporate exercise in your life, this could be a time to see if there's a way to challenge yourself and take it up a level or pick new activities you'd like to add to the mix. Maybe you've always wanted to try martial arts or pilates. Also, check and see if you're only focusing on one area. Perhaps you've only been doing cardio and need to add some strength training and stretching.

If exercise isn't a part of your life, bring it in. I want you to go easy on yourself and start slowly building on your progress. Pick an activity in each area and every couple of weeks push yourself a little more. Let's say you pick walking as your cardio. You could begin with just a ten minute walk. Then add five minutes every week or two until you reach your targeted amount of time. When beginning an exercise routine, especially if you have any health concerns, it's a good idea talk to your doctor first.

Choose an activity for each area below keeping in mind your preferences above. I'll list some suggestions, but don't limit yourself to them. Pick what works for you. You can also select a few ideas to give yourself some variety. As you pick activities, think about how many days you want to devote to each area. You can combine each area into a longer workout a few days a week. You can rotate and focus on one area each day. Again, the key is to pick a schedule that will work for you and you can commit to doing. You'll plug these into the calendar at the end of the chapter.

(Cardio Ideas: walking, running, biking, swimming, aerobic YouTube videos, dancing, joining a soccer team, or an aerobic class at a gym)

*My cardio exercise(s):*_____

*Days per week:*_____

(Strength Training Ideas: pushups/sit ups/squats/lunges, free weights with a YouTube video, kettle ball exercises, or strength training with a personal trainer)

*My strength training exercise(s):*_____

*Days per week:*_____

(Stretching/Flexibility Ideas: yoga videos on YouTube, a yoga class, or general stretching incorporated with cardio and strength training exercises)

*My stretching/flexibility exercise(s):*_____

*Days per week:*_____

Nutrition

You've probably heard the saying you are what you eat. It's true. Nutrition is a vast area to dive into. Looking into the research and optimizing your diet is a game changer in how you feel and in your overall health. Like I said at the beginning of this chapter, each person is unique and has different and changing needs, especially in the area of nutrition, so I'm going to just give you some tips that have helped me. If you're interested in diving deeper into the subject of nutrition, I'll recommend some resources to start you off. The book *31-Day Food Revolution: Heal Your Body, Feel Great, and Transform Your World* by Ocean Robbins along with the Food Revolution Network at https://www.foodrevolution.org are fantastic, especially if you're interested in a vegetarian or vegan diet. If including animal protein in your diet is a better fit for you, Dr. Mark Hyman's books such as *Food: What the Heck Should I Eat?* and *The Pegan Diet: 21 Practical Principles for Reclaiming Your Health in a Nutritionally Confusing World* are also great. And finally, *Fiber Fueled: The Plant-Based Gut Health Program for Losing Weight, Restoring Your Health, and Optimizing Your Microbiome* along with *The Fiber Fueled Cookbook: Inspiring Plant-Based Recipes to Turbocharge Your Health* by Will Bulsiewicz, MD are amazing guides to a healthy diet. If you have special health circumstances, food sensitivities, or food allergies, consult with your doctor and/or a nutritionist to personalize your diet for your needs but, for now, onto some basic principles to get you going.

First, make sure you're staying hydrated. A general rule is for women to get eleven and a half cups (2.7 liters) and men to get fifteen and a half cups (3.7 liters) of water every day. If you're exercising or are in the heat, you might need more. If you're not drinking enough water, find a way to track how much water you're consuming throughout the day. Fill a pitcher up with the amount you need each morning and drink from it throughout the day, or check off every time you have a cup to monitor your intake. You can add slices of lemons, oranges, cucumber, or mint leaves to flavor your water. Herbal teas are another great way to get your hydration in. A helpful habit is to bring a container of water with you when you go to work or run errands. I recommend using glass or stainless steel containers instead of plastic and to use some type of filtering system for your water.

Next, real food is a key to health. Cut out artificial flavors, colors, and preservatives, and avoid processed food, refined carbohydrates, refined oils, and added sugar as much as possible.

So, what should this real food consist of? Eat a wide variety of colorful fruits and vegetables, legumes, nuts, seeds, herbs, and spices, making sure to get some healthy sources of protein, good fats, and whole grains. I'd also recommend incorporating some food sources that contain probiotics. Following are lists of some options in each area to get you started.

Fruits

Blueberries	Grapefruit	Pineapple
Strawberries	Apples	Mangos
Raspberries	Pears	Peaches
Blackberries	Pomegranates	Bananas
Cherries	Kiwi	Figs
Cranberries	Grapes	Dragon fruit
Goji berries	Watermelon	Jack fruit
Acai	Cantaloupe	Passion fruit
Oranges	Papaya	Kumquats

Vegetables
(A few are technically not vegetables, but are typically prepared and eaten like vegetables.)

Greens (arugula, spinach, dandelion greens, kale, bok choy, rainbow chard, & collards)	Onions	Cauliflower
	Shallots	Sweet potatoes
	Garlic	Artichokes
	Brocoli	Asparagus
Mushrooms *always cook	Brocoli sprouts	Turnips

Health

Radishes	Jicama root	Seaweed
Beets	Jerusalem artichoke	Butternut squash
Fennel	Leeks	Zucchini
Carrots	Purple cabbage	Tomatoes
Celery	Brussels sprouts	Bell peppers (*red, yellow,*
Watercress	Turnips	*& green*)

Legumes

Beans	Lentils	Soybeans
Chickpeas	Peas	Peanuts

Nuts, Seeds, & Other Healthy Fats

Walnuts	Pine nuts	Olives
Almonds	Flax seeds *grind	Avocados
Brazil nuts	Chia seeds	Wild caught salmon
Pecans	Hemp seeds	Herring
Hazelnuts	Pumpkin seeds	Sardines
Macadamia nuts	Sunflower seeds	Anchovies

Protein

If you eat meat, lean, unprocessed cuts	Wild caught salmon	Amaranth
Egg whites	Soy (*tofu, tempeh, &*	Beans & lentils combined with rice
Sardines	*edamame*)	Nutritional yeast
Anchovies	Quinoa	Spirulina with grains, oats, nuts, or seeds

Grains

Buckwheat (*It's really a seed that can be used like a grain.*)	Millet	Spelt
	Quinoa	Teff
Whole oats (*rolled, steel cut, & oat groats*)	Kamut	Brown rice
	Bulgur wheat	Corn

Herbs, Spices, & Teas

Basil	Tarragon	Ginger
Rosemary	Mint	Green tea
Oregano	Cinnamon	Matcha tea
Thyme	Cardamom	Black tea
Sage	Chili powder	White tea
Parsley	Coriander	Chai tea
Cilantro	Paprika	Chamomile tea
Chives	Turmeric	Various herbal teas

Probiotics

Sauerkraut	Kimchi	Tempeh (*cook*)
Pickles (*Buy pickles sold in the refrigerated section that say intact for probiotics.*)	Miso	Puer tea (*also spelled pu'erh*)
	Yogurt	Raw apple cider vinegar
	Kefir	Kombucha

Another tip is to give your digestive system some down time. Don't eat constantly throughout the day and keep you meals to healthy portions. You don't want to starve yourself, but you don't want to make yourself feel stuffed either. Focus on feeling satisfied. Try having your last meal earlier rather than later. About three to four hours before you go to bed is great. Also, try giving your digestive system a rest between your last and first meal. Going twelve to fourteen hours will have positive effects for most people. If you're pregnant, nursing, diabetic, or have some other special circumstance, going too long without eating might not be advisable. Talk with your doctor and listen to your body.

Just like with exercise, you have to start where you are. Don't try to go from eating zero fruits and vegetables to eating eight in one day, or from no legumes in your diet to legumes at every meal. You'll give your digestive system quite a shock. Each week try swapping out one unhealthy item with a healthy option from the list above and build on that adding more with each coming week, and try one new healthy recipe each week. Once your system is used to a good amount of fruits and vegetables, smoothies, salads, and soups are great ways to get a wide variety of healthy food in. One more idea for healthy eating is to plan ahead each week and have fresh food available.

With all that said, I'm going to add that food should be a pleasurable experience. Find healthy recipes that you actually enjoy. If you don't like what you're eating, you're not going to stick to it. Make meal times a beautiful and special event. Set the table. Add flowers and candles. Appreciate and give thanks for the food. Think of all that went into getting the food from a seed to your plate. Think of the nutrition the food is providing you. Incorporate all your senses as you eat. Bonus… this is a great way to practice presence. Also, it's not an all or nothing deal. Just like eating food you don't like won't stick, feeling like you're depriving yourself won't work either. It's okay to have a treat. Just don't make it every meal, and try to keep it natural. A homemade dessert is far better than some packaged processed doughnut. A gourmet dark chocolate bar is far better than a bag of artificially colored, artificially flavored sugary candy. For a lot of people, food can be a difficult area. If you feel like food is something you struggle with, the help of a nutritionist or a counselor may be a good investment.

On the calendar add an unhealthy food to cut out and a healthy food replacement along with one new recipe to try each week.

Stress Reduction

Stress is an unavoidable part of life, but chronic stress has negative effects on health. We all need to find ways to address and manage stressors in our lives.

Start by taking a look at your daily life. Are there circumstances that fill you with stress and anxiety? Can these circumstances be addressed and changed? We get stuck in routines and sometimes need to step back and see how we can adjust our daily schedules to work for us. For example, if mornings are filled with rushing and the feeling of not having enough time/being late, adjust your schedule. Wake up ten or fifteen minutes earlier. Set your clothes out. If you're making breakfast(s) and/or lunch(es), prepare them ahead. Perhaps specific people are adding stress to your life. Ask yourself how these relationships can be addressed and changed or if they should simply be cut out of your life. Take some time to reflect on stressors in your life and think about ways you can adjust them. Then list your stressors and adjustments you can make.

Health

Stressor *Adjustment I can make*

Now that you've looked at ways to address some of your stressors, let's look at ways to deal with the stress that remains. Breath work, yoga, tai chi, meditation, time outdoors, exercise, and therapy are all healthy ways to deal with stress. The presence activity you picked in the spirit chapter can be combined as your stress release activity or you can pick an additional activity. Pick and write down what you'd like to try.

*My stress release activity:*_____

"Hang-Ups"

When I say "hang-ups," I'm referring to a wide range of activities that negatively impact you. "Hang-ups" can range from habits all the way to addictions. They could be biting your nails, eating too much junk, smoking, drinking too much, or even illegal drugs. I want you to take an honest look at your life and self. If you are controlled by actions that have a negative impact, they will take you off track from your targets. If you feel you have a "hang-up" you can stop on your own, it may be as simple as becoming aware and actively choosing not to do it or replacing it with a healthy habit. If you feel you cannot stop something that is negatively impacting your life, you must get help. Talk to your doctor to get a referral or call one of the resources I've listed below. You don't want something controlling you. You want to be in charge of yourself. Take time and reflect on any "hang-up" or "hang-ups" and come up with a plan to address it or them.

Resources for help…

1. Substance Abuse and Mental Health Service Administration
    Phone: 1-800-662-4357
    Website: https://samhsa.gov
2. Help Guide
    Website: https://www.helpguide.org

Health

"Hang-up"	*My plan to address it*

Health Target

Now it's time to get clear about where you want to be in the element of health and set your target. Review your revised list at the beginning of this chapter. What do you want your life to be like in this element? Take some time to reflect and then set your target below remembering to be very specific.

◎

Just as you did with your spirit target, create a plan to reach your health target with small steps. Again, some of the practices suggested in the chapter might even be steps.

Target Your Life

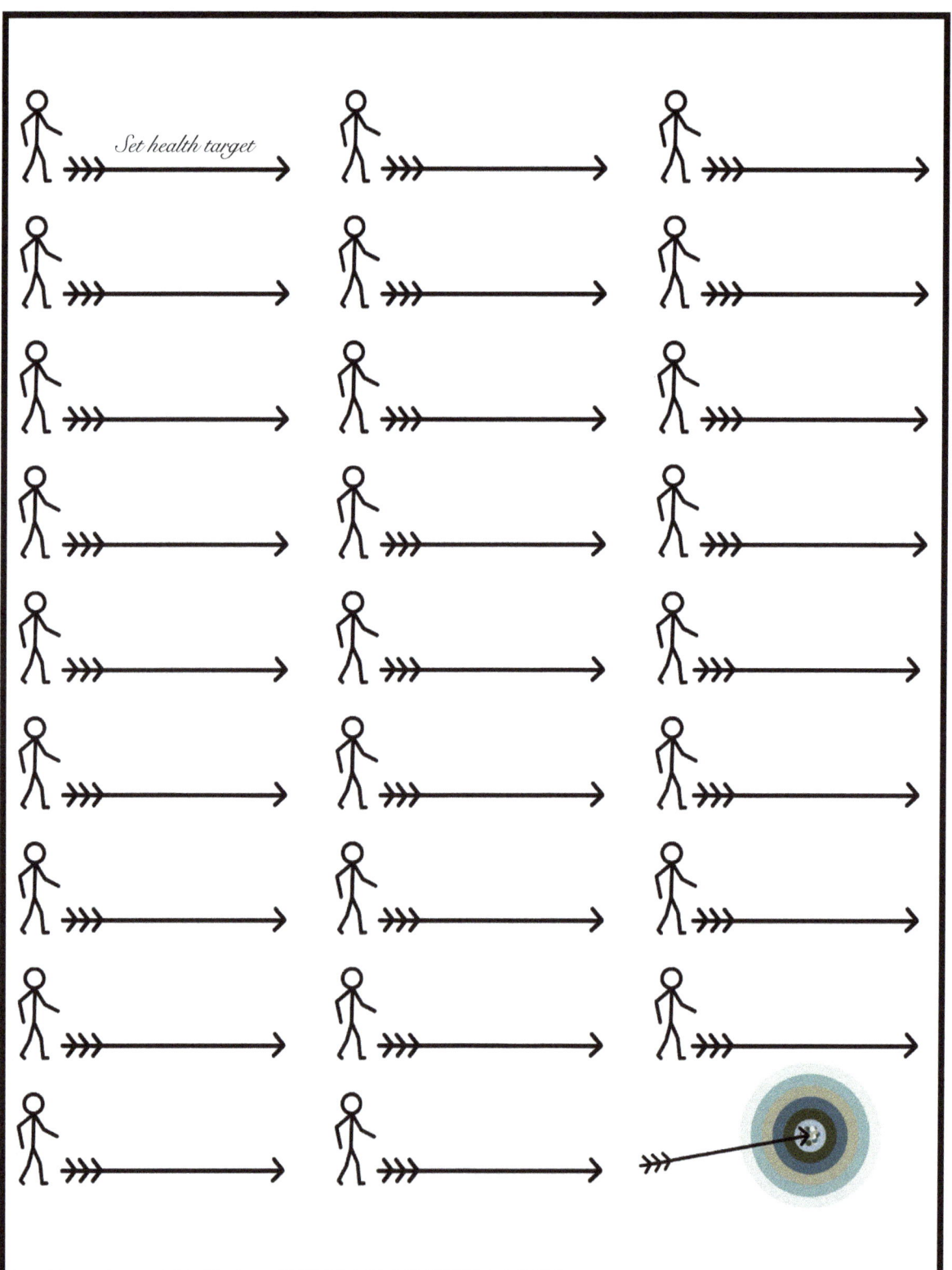

38

Taking Aim with Actions

Now you'll build on the action calendar from the first chapter. I want you to keep up your spirit practices and add your health practices along with small steps toward your targets.

Schedule in…

- Your giving activity
- Your random act of kindness
- Your spiritual practice
- Your forgiveness check (Do you need to forgive yourself or anyone else?)
- Your cardio, strength, and stretching/flexibility exercises for each week
- Any stressors or "hang-ups" to be addressed

Pick at least 1 step toward your target for each element & schedule…

Spirit:_____

Health:_____

Health

	Sunday	Monday	Tuesday	Wednesday	Thursday	Friday	Saturday	*Reward*
Week 1	__ AM, Noon, & PM: Close your eyes, picture presence image, and take 3 slow, deep breaths __ Stay hydrated __ Presence activity/stress release activity __ Gratitude journal __ To sleep at bedtime *Healthy food swap for the week:* *Healthy recipe to try this week:*	__ AM, Noon, & PM: Close your eyes, picture presence image, and take 3 slow, deep breaths __ Stay hydrated __ Presence activity/stress release activity __ Gratitude journal __ To sleep at bedtime	__ AM, Noon, & PM: Close your eyes, picture presence image, and take 3 slow, deep breaths __ Stay hydrated __ Presence activity/stress release activity __ Gratitude journal __ To sleep at bedtime	__ AM, Noon, & PM: Close your eyes, picture presence image, and take 3 slow, deep breaths __ Stay hydrated __ Presence activity/stress release activity __ Gratitude journal __ To sleep at bedtime	__ AM, Noon, & PM: Close your eyes, picture presence image, and take 3 slow, deep breaths __ Stay hydrated __ Presence activity/stress release activity __ Gratitude journal __ To sleep at bedtime	__ AM, Noon, & PM: Close your eyes, picture presence image, and take 3 slow, deep breaths __ Stay hydrated __ Presence activity/stress release activity __ Gratitude journal __ To sleep at bedtime	__ AM, Noon, & PM: Close your eyes, picture presence image, and take 3 slow, deep breaths __ Stay hydrated __ Presence activity/stress release activity __ Gratitude journal __ To sleep at bedtime	🎁
Week 2	__ AM, Noon, & PM: Close your eyes, picture presence image, and take 3 slow, deep breaths __ Stay hydrated __ Presence activity/stress release activity __ Gratitude journal __ To sleep at bedtime *Healthy food swap for the week:* *Healthy recipe to try this week:*	__ AM, Noon, & PM: Close your eyes, picture presence image, and take 3 slow, deep breaths __ Stay hydrated __ Presence activity/stress release activity __ Gratitude journal __ To sleep at bedtime	__ AM, Noon, & PM: Close your eyes, picture presence image, and take 3 slow, deep breaths __ Stay hydrated __ Presence activity/stress release activity __ Gratitude journal __ To sleep at bedtime	__ AM, Noon, & PM: Close your eyes, picture presence image, and take 3 slow, deep breaths __ Stay hydrated __ Presence activity/stress release activity __ Gratitude journal __ To sleep at bedtime	__ AM, Noon, & PM: Close your eyes, picture presence image, and take 3 slow, deep breaths __ Stay hydrated __ Presence activity/stress release activity __ Gratitude journal __ To sleep at bedtime	__ AM, Noon, & PM: Close your eyes, picture presence image, and take 3 slow, deep breaths __ Stay hydrated __ Presence activity/stress release activity __ Gratitude journal __ To sleep at bedtime	__ AM, Noon, & PM: Close your eyes, picture presence image, and take 3 slow, deep breaths __ Stay hydrated __ Presence activity/stress release activity __ Gratitude journal __ To sleep at bedtime	🎁

Daily Spirit Reminders…

- Focus on the positive
- Express gratitude
- Shift your perspective on obligations as an opportunity to give

Health

	Sunday	Monday	Tuesday	Wednesday	Thursday	Friday	Saturday	*Reward*
Week 3	__ AM, Noon, & PM: Close your eyes, picture presence image, and take 3 slow, deep breaths __ Stay hydrated __ Presence activity/stress release activity __ Gratitude journal __ To sleep at bedtime --- --- --- --- *Healthy food swap for the week:* *Healthy recipe to try this week:*	__ AM, Noon, & PM: Close your eyes, picture presence image, and take 3 slow, deep breaths __ Stay hydrated __ Presence activity/stress release activity __ Gratitude journal __ To sleep at bedtime	__ AM, Noon, & PM: Close your eyes, picture presence image, and take 3 slow, deep breaths __ Stay hydrated __ Presence activity/stress release activity __ Gratitude journal __ To sleep at bedtime	__ AM, Noon, & PM: Close your eyes, picture presence image, and take 3 slow, deep breaths __ Stay hydrated __ Presence activity/stress release activity __ Gratitude journal __ To sleep at bedtime	__ AM, Noon, & PM: Close your eyes, picture presence image, and take 3 slow, deep breaths __ Stay hydrated __ Presence activity/stress release activity __ Gratitude journal __ To sleep at bedtime	__ AM, Noon, & PM: Close your eyes, picture presence image, and take 3 slow, deep breaths __ Stay hydrated __ Presence activity/stress release activity __ Gratitude journal __ To sleep at bedtime	__ AM, Noon, & PM: Close your eyes, picture presence image, and take 3 slow, deep breaths __ Stay hydrated __ Presence activity/stress release activity __ Gratitude journal __ To sleep at bedtime	🎁
Week 4	__ AM, Noon, & PM: Close your eyes, picture presence image, and take 3 slow, deep breaths __ Stay hydrated __ Presence activity/stress release activity __ Gratitude journal __ To sleep at bedtime --- --- --- --- *Healthy food swap for the week:* *Healthy recipe to try this week:*	__ AM, Noon, & PM: Close your eyes, picture presence image, and take 3 slow, deep breaths __ Stay hydrated __ Presence activity/stress release activity __ Gratitude journal __ To sleep at bedtime	__ AM, Noon, & PM: Close your eyes, picture presence image, and take 3 slow, deep breaths __ Stay hydrated __ Presence activity/stress release activity __ Gratitude journal __ To sleep at bedtime	__ AM, Noon, & PM: Close your eyes, picture presence image, and take 3 slow, deep breaths __ Stay hydrated __ Presence activity/stress release activity __ Gratitude journal __ To sleep at bedtime	__ AM, Noon, & PM: Close your eyes, picture presence image, and take 3 slow, deep breaths __ Stay hydrated __ Presence activity/stress release activity __ Gratitude journal __ To sleep at bedtime	__ AM, Noon, & PM: Close your eyes, picture presence image, and take 3 slow, deep breaths __ Stay hydrated __ Presence activity/stress release activity __ Gratitude journal __ To sleep at bedtime	__ AM, Noon, & PM: Close your eyes, picture presence image, and take 3 slow, deep breaths __ Stay hydrated __ Presence activity/stress release activity __ Gratitude journal __ To sleep at bedtime	🎁

Daily Health Reminders…

- Eat real, unprocessed food
- Finish eating 3 to 4 hours before bed
- Go 12 to 14 hours between last and first meal

PRESENTATION

What do I mean by presentation? I mean how you're presenting yourself to the world. As you move forward in life, I recommend reviewing the elements and your targets as needed. Presentation is the one I need to revisit the most. Some people are naturals at this. Not me. If I let it slide, I really let it slide. For example, when I was staying at home with my young son, I was Skyping my sister one morning and caught a glimpse of myself on the computer screen. I have naturally frizzy hair and didn't bother fixing it after a shower the night before. My hair was all over the place. I also happened to be wearing glasses that were missing one of the ear pieces my son had broken off. So they were hanging by one ear slanted on my face. To top it off, I was wearing a robe that had taken a tumble session in the dryer with some crayons I had picked up off the ground and stuffed in the pockets forgetting to take them out for the wash. It looked like a bad tie dye job…Yikes!

Presentation is a tricky one in our society. We are bombarded with images that are not real, and they often make us feel like we have to be perfect. That's not what I'm talking about here. I'm talking about trying and feeling good. Clearly, I was not making any effort in the scene I described above. When you put in the effort to pull yourself together, keep yourself groomed, and wear clothes that fit and you like, you feel better and more confident. So let's talk about ways to do this. Before we get going, list where you feel your presentation is off track and then post the opposite words over them.

Grooming

Just like people have to straighten and clean their home, you've got to keep yourself up. The following are some basic practices that will keep you groomed and pulled together. Many of them are pretty obvious, but there might be a few reminders of areas you're letting go. Like I said earlier, when you present the best version of yourself, it gives you a boost of confidence and just makes you feel better. We will dive deeper into cleaning, organizing, and making our spaces more uplifting in a couple chapters, but as you reflect on your grooming, you can get a jump on this. Are there expired products or products you don't use that need to go? Could your bathroom use a bit of cleaning and organizing?

Daily Basics	Daily Bonuses
* Brush your teeth at least twice a day * Floss your teeth at least once a day * Keep yourself clean * Check your nails for touch ups * Shave etc. as needed * Style your hair * Moisturize (face, body, & lips) * Wear sunscreen (hats & sunglasses add protection)	* Wear a perfume or cologne that you love * Dry brush before you bathe or shower * Buff any rough spots on your feet * Use cuticle oil * Use a tongue scraper * Put on makeup if you wear it

Weekly Basics	Weekly Bonuses
* Either give yourself or get a manicure and pedicure (You don't have to polish if you're not into that, but you want to keep your nails tidy.)	* Exfoliate your face and body * Use a face mask for your needs * Use a deep conditioning hair treatment

Monthly Basics	Monthly Bonuses
* Clean your hair and makeup brushes * Trim your hair (every few months/as needed) * Change your toothbrush every few months	* If you color or highlight your hair, keep that up as needed * Whiten teeth as needed * Spa treatments

Check in and see if you're letting any area in your grooming slide. As a side note, the more natural grooming products may be better. Your skin absorbs what you put on it. Many products are filled with harmful ingredients. Check out the Environmental Working Group's Skin Deep cosmetic data base at https://www.ewg.org/skindeep/ for recommendations.

Grooming area I've let slide	*Actions to address*
_____	_____
_____	_____
_____	_____
_____	_____
_____	_____
_____	_____
_____	_____
_____	_____
_____	_____
_____	_____
_____	_____
_____	_____
_____	_____
_____	_____
_____	_____
_____	_____
_____	_____
_____	_____

Now take time to get some inspiration. Would you like a big change or to fine tune your appearance? Look through magazines, Pinterest, or something of that sort. What would you like your hair to look like? If you're not sure, you could ask advice from a stylist. What color would look best on you? What cut would complement your face and hair texture? You want to work with what you've got, not against it. Next, if you wear makeup, find some pictures you'd like to recreate for everyday and special occasions. You could even go to a makeup artist and get his/her advice and some techniques for applying. As you're doing this, consider how much time you have and want to put into getting ready. Some people are willing to spend an hour of their day on hair and makeup. Some people would prefer ten minutes. Pick what works for you. Use your images and describe your vision for your appearance along with steps to achieve it.

Vision for my appearance	*Steps to achieve vision*

Clothes

Do you like your clothes? Do they reflect your style? Do they fit well and are they comfortable? Many people go into their closet and feel like they have nothing to wear or what they have doesn't fit or look good on them. If you find yourself feeling like this, let's fix that.

Clothes can be expensive. So, giving away all your clothes and buying a whole new wardrobe isn't a practical option. With that in mind, I'll let you know what worked for me. For the first step, you'll need to clear some time to do an assessment. Go through all of your clothes. I mean everything from jewelry, purses, wallets, scarves, hats, and jackets to shoes, underwear, and socks and everything else in between. I want you to sort everything into four different piles. The first pile is for items that have holes and are falling apart. These are items you can't even give away. Next, make a pile for items that do not fit or when you put them on make you feel self-conscious. Now, make a pile for items that aren't your favorite, but they fit. After all you do have to wear something. Finally, make a pile for the clothes you love. Alright, here's what I want you to do with your first two piles…

Holes/are falling apart…To the trash or a fabric recycling center
Do not fit/make you feel self-conscious…To a donation center

For the last two piles, find a way to divide your closet and drawers into two sections. One will be for the items you love and will keep. The other will be for the things you're keeping for now until you find replacements that can be moved to the love section. This is also a good time to make sure your closet and drawers are clean and organized. Depending on your budget, you may just replace one item a month. If that's still too much of a strain on your budget, just save up and replace as you can. If you can replace more at a time, go for it. Just don't buy anything that doesn't fit and doesn't make you feel good. Remember, you're going to be putting these new items into the section you love. It's okay if it takes time to save for and find the items. Don't forget about having clothes tailored as well. That can make a huge difference in how something fits. The goal is to have a closet filled with items you actually like, reflect your style, fit well, and are comfortable. Each time you find a replacement, give away what you're replacing from your keeping for now section.

I also recommend making sure you have all the basics you need. Here is a general list to check through. Be sure to factor in your work, daily activities, hobbies, and climate. And, if you're like me and style doesn't come naturally, you can even use this list and find some pictures that inspire you to recreate for yourself. I've left some space to make notes if needed.

* Underwear/bras
_____
_____
_____

* Socks
_____
_____

* Sleepwear/loungewear
_____
_____
_____

* Bathing suit/cover up etc. (if you swim or go to the beach)
_____
_____
_____

* Camisoles/undershirts
_____
_____
_____

* Accessories (jewelry, purse, wallet, sunglasses, hats, umbrella etc.)
_____
_____
_____

* Coats/gloves/scarves
_____
_____
_____

* Clothes/shoes to work out in (check for all seasons)
_____
_____
_____

* Everyday clothes/shoes (check for all seasons)
_____
_____
_____

* Work clothes/shoes (check for all seasons)
_____
_____
_____

* Special occasion clothes/shoes (check for all seasons)
_____
_____

(With jeans and pants, if you wear heels sometimes, make sure you have lengths for both heels and flats.)

Stance

Okay, you're on your way with your grooming and clothes. Before we move on from presentation to the next element, let's take a minute and think about how our body language affects our presentation. If someone walks into a room hunched over, frowning, looking at the ground with their arms crossed, they will give off a very different energy than someone coming into a room with good posture, smiling with their head held high making eye contact. Which energy would you like to emit? My guess is the latter. This may take practice. If you're shy, it might take more effort and require you to fake it till you make it. The more you make the effort to stand or sit up straight, make eye contact, and smile, the more it will become a natural habit. It will positively boost your confidence and the way others perceive you. Throughout the day check in often and see where you fall in your stance and make adjustments as needed. I've left some space for notes if you'd like to write down what you're noticing or working on.

Slouched vs. Spine straight, shoulders back, and head held high
Frowning vs. Smiling
Looking at the ground, etc. vs. Making eye contact
Arms crossed vs. Arms relaxed

Presentation Target

Where do you want to be in the element of presentation? Review your revised list at the beginning of this chapter, the images you found, and the notes you made. Take some time to reflect and then set your target below.

Once again, think about what it will take to achieve your presentation target and break the path to your target into steps.

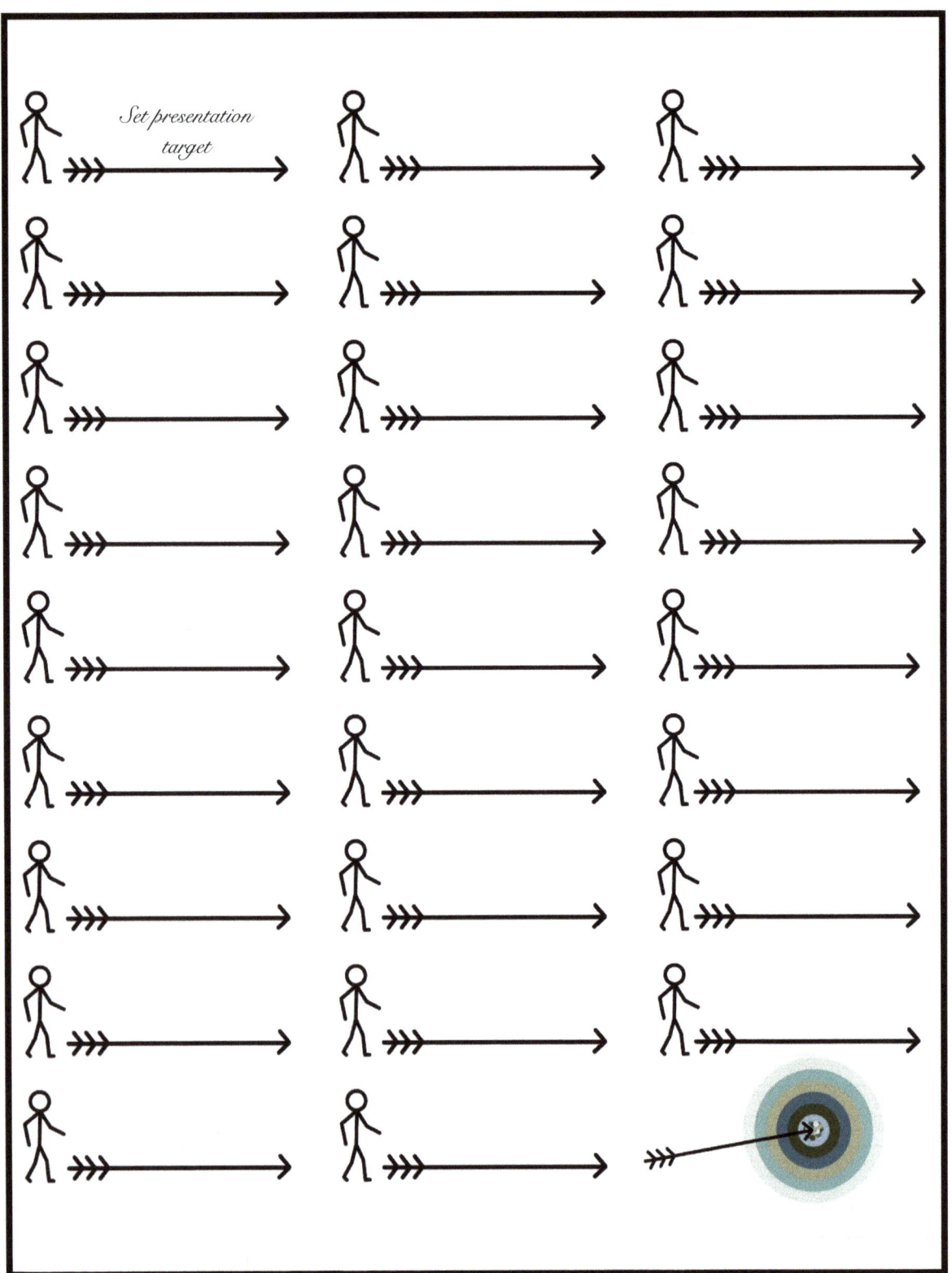

Taking Aim with Actions

Continuing with your spirit and health practices, add your presentation practices along with small steps toward your targets.

Schedule in…

- Your giving activity
- Your random act of kindness
- Your spiritual practice
- Your forgiveness check (Do you need to forgive yourself or anyone else?)
- Your cardio, strength, and stretching/flexibility exercises for each week
- Any stressors or "hang-ups" to be addressed
- Hair inspiration/ execution
- Makeup inspiration/ execution (if applicable)
- Time to clean out bathroom products
- Clothes assessment
- Time to take items to donate and throw out/recycle
- Time to organize clothes

Pick at least 1 step toward your target for each element & schedule…

Spirit:_____

Health:_____

Presentation:_____

Presentation

	Sunday	Monday	Tuesday	Wednesday	Thursday	Friday	Saturday	*Reward*
Week 1	__ AM, Noon, & PM: Close your eyes, picture presence image, and take 3 slow, deep breaths __ Stay hydrated __ Presence activity/stress release activity __ Gratitude journal __ To sleep at bedtime *Healthy food swap for the week:* *Healthy recipe to try this week:*	__ AM, Noon, & PM: Close your eyes, picture presence image, and take 3 slow, deep breaths __ Stay hydrated __ Presence activity/stress release activity __ Gratitude journal __ To sleep at bedtime	__ AM, Noon, & PM: Close your eyes, picture presence image, and take 3 slow, deep breaths __ Stay hydrated __ Presence activity/stress release activity __ Gratitude journal __ To sleep at bedtime	__ AM, Noon, & PM: Close your eyes, picture presence image, and take 3 slow, deep breaths __ Stay hydrated __ Presence activity/stress release activity __ Gratitude journal __ To sleep at bedtime	__ AM, Noon, & PM: Close your eyes, picture presence image, and take 3 slow, deep breaths __ Stay hydrated __ Presence activity/stress release activity __ Gratitude journal __ To sleep at bedtime	__ AM, Noon, & PM: Close your eyes, picture presence image, and take 3 slow, deep breaths __ Stay hydrated __ Presence activity/stress release activity __ Gratitude journal __ To sleep at bedtime	__ AM, Noon, & PM: Close your eyes, picture presence image, and take 3 slow, deep breaths __ Stay hydrated __ Presence activity/stress release activity __ Gratitude journal __ To sleep at bedtime	🎁
Week 2	__ AM, Noon, & PM: Close your eyes, picture presence image, and take 3 slow, deep breaths __ Stay hydrated __ Presence activity/stress release activity __ Gratitude journal __ To sleep at bedtime *Healthy food swap for the week:* *Healthy recipe to try this week:*	__ AM, Noon, & PM: Close your eyes, picture presence image, and take 3 slow, deep breaths __ Stay hydrated __ Presence activity/stress release activity __ Gratitude journal __ To sleep at bedtime	__ AM, Noon, & PM: Close your eyes, picture presence image, and take 3 slow, deep breaths __ Stay hydrated __ Presence activity/stress release activity __ Gratitude journal __ To sleep at bedtime	__ AM, Noon, & PM: Close your eyes, picture presence image, and take 3 slow, deep breaths __ Stay hydrated __ Presence activity/stress release activity __ Gratitude journal __ To sleep at bedtime	__ AM, Noon, & PM: Close your eyes, picture presence image, and take 3 slow, deep breaths __ Stay hydrated __ Presence activity/stress release activity __ Gratitude journal __ To sleep at bedtime	__ AM, Noon, & PM: Close your eyes, picture presence image, and take 3 slow, deep breaths __ Stay hydrated __ Presence activity/stress release activity __ Gratitude journal __ To sleep at bedtime	__ AM, Noon, & PM: Close your eyes, picture presence image, and take 3 slow, deep breaths __ Stay hydrated __ Presence activity/stress release activity __ Gratitude journal __ To sleep at bedtime	🎁

Daily Spirit Reminders...

- Focus on the positive
- Express gratitude
- Shift your perspective on obligations as an opportunity to give

Daily Health Reminders...

- Eat real, unprocessed food
- Finish eating 3 to 4 hours before bed
- Go 12 to 14 hours between last and first meal

Presentation

	Sunday	Monday	Tuesday	Wednesday	Thursday	Friday	Saturday	*Reward*
Week 3	__ AM, Noon, & PM: Close your eyes, picture presence image, and take 3 slow, deep breaths __ Stay hydrated __ Presence activity/stress release activity __ Gratitude journal __ To sleep at bedtime *Healthy food swap for the week:* *Healthy recipe to try this week:*	__ AM, Noon, & PM: Close your eyes, picture presence image, and take 3 slow, deep breaths __ Stay hydrated __ Presence activity/stress release activity __ Gratitude journal __ To sleep at bedtime	__ AM, Noon, & PM: Close your eyes, picture presence image, and take 3 slow, deep breaths __ Stay hydrated __ Presence activity/stress release activity __ Gratitude journal __ To sleep at bedtime	__ AM, Noon, & PM: Close your eyes, picture presence image, and take 3 slow, deep breaths __ Stay hydrated __ Presence activity/stress release activity __ Gratitude journal __ To sleep at bedtime	__ AM, Noon, & PM: Close your eyes, picture presence image, and take 3 slow, deep breaths __ Stay hydrated __ Presence activity/stress release activity __ Gratitude journal __ To sleep at bedtime	__ AM, Noon, & PM: Close your eyes, picture presence image, and take 3 slow, deep breaths __ Stay hydrated __ Presence activity/stress release activity __ Gratitude journal __ To sleep at bedtime	__ AM, Noon, & PM: Close your eyes, picture presence image, and take 3 slow, deep breaths __ Stay hydrated __ Presence activity/stress release activity __ Gratitude journal __ To sleep at bedtime	🎁
Week 4	__ AM, Noon, & PM: Close your eyes, picture presence image, and take 3 slow, deep breaths __ Stay hydrated __ Presence activity/stress release activity __ Gratitude journal __ To sleep at bedtime *Healthy food swap for the week:* *Healthy recipe to try this week:*	__ AM, Noon, & PM: Close your eyes, picture presence image, and take 3 slow, deep breaths __ Stay hydrated __ Presence activity/stress release activity __ Gratitude journal __ To sleep at bedtime	__ AM, Noon, & PM: Close your eyes, picture presence image, and take 3 slow, deep breaths __ Stay hydrated __ Presence activity/stress release activity __ Gratitude journal __ To sleep at bedtime	__ AM, Noon, & PM: Close your eyes, picture presence image, and take 3 slow, deep breaths __ Stay hydrated __ Presence activity/stress release activity __ Gratitude journal __ To sleep at bedtime	__ AM, Noon, & PM: Close your eyes, picture presence image, and take 3 slow, deep breaths __ Stay hydrated __ Presence activity/stress release activity __ Gratitude journal __ To sleep at bedtime	__ AM, Noon, & PM: Close your eyes, picture presence image, and take 3 slow, deep breaths __ Stay hydrated __ Presence activity/stress release activity __ Gratitude journal __ To sleep at bedtime	__ AM, Noon, & PM: Close your eyes, picture presence image, and take 3 slow, deep breaths __ Stay hydrated __ Presence activity/stress release activity __ Gratitude journal __ To sleep at bedtime	🎁

Daily Presentation Reminders…

- Keep up with grooming practices
- Stance check-ins

JOY

The element joy is what life is all about! Sometimes people get so caught up in doing, they forget to make time for joy, or they think once they reach or attain something they'll be able to relax and enjoy their life. We must fill our lives with joy every day. We aren't promised tomorrow. This chapter will be about finding out what brings you joy, pleasure, and fun and incorporating those things into your life each day. It will encompass activities you're passionate about/hobbies, your surroundings, your senses, and your relationships. Start by checking in with where you are in your life with this element. List ways you feel you may be off track and then replace those words with the opposite.

_____
_____
_____
_____
_____
_____
_____
_____
_____
_____

What Brings You Joy?

What brings you joy is a question that will produce different answers for each of us. As we go through this chapter, I want you to think specifically from the perspective of your true self. Don't think of what society or others might say are fun activities or what your friends or family like. Connect with what resonates with you. To start, find a time when you won't be interrupted, make a nice cup of tea or coffee, get comfortable, and collect images that make you happy. You can get some old magazines and glue them to a big piece of paper or do this electronically. Maybe it's the colors that draw you in, the place, the animals, or the activity? Don't over analyze. If it fills you with a joyful feeling, paste it.

Once you have your images, I want you to go through and think about what drew you to each picture and write those thoughts down below.

Colors	Places
_____	_____
_____	_____
_____	_____
_____	_____
_____	_____
_____	_____
_____	_____
_____	_____
_____	_____
_____	_____

Activities	Animals
_____	_____
_____	_____
_____	_____
_____	_____
_____	_____
_____	_____
_____	_____
_____	_____
_____	_____
_____	_____

Objects	Aesthetics
_____	_____
_____	_____
_____	_____
_____	_____
_____	_____
_____	_____
_____	_____
_____	_____
_____	_____
_____	_____

Joy

Feelings   *Sounds and smells*

(Of course you can't feel, hear, or smell a photograph, but the image of a cozy blanket on a chair by a fireplace might make you think of warmth or a person hugging a puppy might make you think of love. Perhaps a photo of a lavender bouquet evokes a relaxing aroma, or maybe someone playing an instrument reminds you of a beautiful melody.)

_____   _____
_____   _____
_____   _____
_____   _____
_____   _____
_____   _____
_____   _____
_____   _____
_____   _____
_____   _____
_____   _____

Other

_____   _____
_____   _____
_____   _____
_____   _____
_____   _____
_____   _____
_____   _____
_____   _____
_____   _____
_____   _____

Now list what you loved and enjoyed doing when you were around ten years old. In general, kids allow themselves to have more fun and gravitate toward what they truly enjoy more than adults do without all the influences and obligations of adulthood. This might spark some pleasures that have been crowed out of your life or you've lost sight of that you might want to bring back into your life.

_____
_____
_____
_____
_____
_____
_____
_____
_____
_____

Passions and Hobbies

Do you already take time to do something you love for the sake of enjoyment? If so, great! Would you like to take it a step further in some way? Maybe join a club or team or take a class to learn more about it. Perhaps you'd like to add some more hobbies to your life. Possibly you haven't been taking time for a hobby. Either way, let's work on finding out what you'd enjoy doing and making time for it in your life. It can feel difficult with obligations such as school, work, or family to make time to do something you enjoy, but it's important.

Alright, think about what you are passionate about and would enjoy doing. You can include things you're already doing as well. Don't limit yourself with this list. Imagine you have the time and ability to do anything you'd like. Write your ideas below.

_____   _____
_____   _____
_____   _____
_____   _____
_____   _____
_____   _____

Now, number the list starting with one for the thing you think would be the most enjoyable and so on. Take your top three and write them below with an idea of what you might do to foster each passion or hobby. Don't feel like you have to give up on the other ideas. You can come back and add them to your life. I just want to get you started. Remember not to exclude things that don't seem possible. You have to work toward your targets, and it may take time. By beginning and taking aim, you can get yourself there. Let's say you find yourself with a passion for gardening and want to have a huge garden, but you live in an apartment right now. Well, you could cultivate a gardening hobby by planting some herbs or vegetables that do well in pots on a balcony or next to a window, read books about gardening, and/or take a gardening class. You could even start a community garden at your apartment complex. Perhaps you would enjoy having and training a dog, but you're renting a home that doesn't allow pets. How about volunteering at an animal shelter? Choose one of your top three passions/hobbies to start with and commit to giving yourself at least an hour a week for it. If you'd like to schedule more time or do more than one, great! The more the better. Make this work for you. As time goes on, add to and change this as you see fit. Just make sure you're giving yourself time each week for a passion/hobby.

Top three passions/hobbies   *Idea to foster*

_____.........._____

_____.........._____

_____.........._____

Joy

*Passion/hobby:*_____

*Activity to foster:*_____

*Day/time/place:*_____

Of course you don't want to have only one hour a week for enjoyment. Sprinkle joy throughout your day! See the wonder in your everyday experiences and make them enjoyable and special. When it comes down to it, a big part of incorporating joy throughout the day and your life is mindset. There will be positives and negatives in each day. The key is to find and focus on what's good. It may take some practice, but the more you intentionally focus on what's good, the more it will become a habit. Here are some ideas to get you started. I've added some blank spaces at the end for your own ideas.

* Play music you love.
* Add flowers and plants to your space.
* Light candles.
* Set the table beautifully.
* Before you eat, stop and give thanks. Think about everything that went into the food being available for you and how it will nourish your body. Smell the food, notice its colors, and really taste the food as you chew.
* Take a social media and/or technology break.
* Take time to curl up by the fireplace or outside and read something you enjoy.
* Feel the warmth of sunshine.
* Listen to birds singing.
* Pause and take notice of blooming flowers in the spring or colorful leaves on a tree in the fall.
* Have photos and paintings of people, animals, places, and images that uplift you.
* Find simple ways to connect with the seasons and celebrate holidays.

_____
_____
_____
_____
_____
_____
_____
_____
_____
_____
_____
_____
_____
_____
_____

Your Surroundings and Your Senses

Think back to the last chapter's discussion on stance. Just as you give off an energy with your stance, your surroundings give off an energy that affects you. If you're spending your time in places that are a mess, dirty, and filled with colors and objects you don't like, that will hinder the joy you feel. Meanwhile, if your surroundings are clean, organized, and filled with colors and objects you love, that will increase the joy in your life. Make your surroundings lift your spirits. Think about the areas where you spend your time and can change, such as your home, car, and place of work. Do an honest assessment of each below. Write down the places where you spend your time and rank them on a scale from one to five for how clean, organized, uplifting, and beautiful each feel to you below.

*Place:*_____

Clean: 1 (Really needs improvement) 2 (Needs improvement) 3 (Could use a little attention) 4 (Good) 5 (Great)
Organized: 1 (Really needs improvement) 2 (Needs improvement) 3 (Could use a little attention) 4 (Good) 5 (Great)
Uplifting: 1 (Really needs improvement) 2 (Needs improvement) 3 (Could use a little attention) 4 (Good) 5 (Great)
Beautiful: 1 (Really needs improvement) 2 (Needs improvement) 3 (Could use a little attention) 4 (Good) 5 (Great)

*Place:*_____

Clean: 1 (Really needs improvement) 2 (Needs improvement) 3 (Could use a little attention) 4 (Good) 5 (Great)
Organized: 1 (Really needs improvement) 2 (Needs improvement) 3 (Could use a little attention) 4 (Good) 5 (Great)
Uplifting: 1 (Really needs improvement) 2 (Needs improvement) 3 (Could use a little attention) 4 (Good) 5 (Great)
Beautiful: 1 (Really needs improvement) 2 (Needs improvement) 3 (Could use a little attention) 4 (Good) 5 (Great)

*Place:*_____

Clean: 1 (Really needs improvement) 2 (Needs improvement) 3 (Could use a little attention) 4 (Good) 5 (Great)
Organized: 1 (Really needs improvement) 2 (Needs improvement) 3 (Could use a little attention) 4 (Good) 5 (Great)
Uplifting: 1 (Really needs improvement) 2 (Needs improvement) 3 (Could use a little attention) 4 (Good) 5 (Great)
Beautiful: 1 (Really needs improvement) 2 (Needs improvement) 3 (Could use a little attention) 4 (Good) 5 (Great)

*Place:*_____

Clean: 1 (Really needs improvement) 2 (Needs improvement) 3 (Could use a little attention) 4 (Good) 5 (Great)
Organized: 1 (Really needs improvement) 2 (Needs improvement) 3 (Could use a little attention) 4 (Good) 5 (Great)
Uplifting: 1 (Really needs improvement) 2 (Needs improvement) 3 (Could use a little attention) 4 (Good) 5 (Great)
Beautiful: 1 (Really needs improvement) 2 (Needs improvement) 3 (Could use a little attention) 4 (Good) 5 (Great)

Now, I want you to reflect on these spaces and think of ways to improve them. Do you need to schedule some time to clean and organize? Could some of your spaces use objects that uplift and inspire you, or could something beautiful bring more joy to your surroundings? This is a great place to incorporate your five senses. Nurturing your senses in your surroundings will help you sprinkle joy throughout the day. Think of sights, smells, sounds, textures, and even tastes (i.e. bowls of fruit in the kitchen) that bring you joy and find ways to add those to your surroundings.

Below, list some ways you could make each space bring you more joy. Remember, just like everything in this book, this process takes time and is always evolving. Don't feel you have to make your space perfect overnight. For example, perhaps the thought of a cozy log cabin in the mountains fills you with joy. If that's not possible at the present moment, you could find a painting or photo of the mountains and diffuse some pine tree oil. Make it a practice to assess your spaces every once in a while because our tastes change as we change.

*Place:*_____

How can I make this space clean and organized?

_____

How can I make this space uplifting and beautiful? (Remember to think of your five senses: sight, smell, sound, touch, and taste!)

_____

*Place:*_____

How can I make this space clean and organized?

_____
_____
_____
_____
_____
_____
_____
_____
_____
_____

How can I make this space uplifting and beautiful? (Remember to think of your five senses: sight, smell, sound, touch, and taste!)

_____
_____
_____
_____
_____
_____
_____
_____
_____
_____

*Place:*_____

How can I make this space clean and organized?

_____
_____
_____
_____
_____
_____
_____
_____
_____
_____

How can I make this space uplifting and beautiful? (Remember to think of your five senses: sight, smell, sound, touch, and taste!)

_____
_____

Place:_____

How can I make this space clean and organized?

How can I make this space uplifting and beautiful? (Remember to think of your five senses: sight, smell, sound, touch, and taste!)

Relationships

Choose who you surround yourself with carefully and make sure you are in fact choosing. Relationships are so important in life, but if they are negative, they will have a negative effect on you. Your relationships should be positive and loving. You should always be able to be your honest and true self. They should lift you up, not drain you. They should be filled with gratitude and appreciation. Consider how the habits and actions of the people you spend your time with influence you. Make sure your relationships are in alignment with your core values and targets, not to say you have to think and be exactly like those in your life. The more perspectives and variety the better. At the same time, if you are trying to get to a target of optimal health, hanging around drug addicts is not the way to go. That's a bit extreme, but you get the idea. You want to be around people who raise the bar and inspire you, not the opposite.

Notice how you feel after talking to or being around different people in your life. If you feel positive (energized, heard, supported, loved etc.), that's a sign it's a relationship to nurture and keep. If you feel negative (drained, agitated, disrespected, taken advantage of etc.), that's a sign it's a relationship that needs honest dialog, counseling, or perhaps ending. If you feel you need more positive relationships in your life, joining groups or taking classes that interest you and volunteering are great ways to meet people with similar interests and values.

Romantic relationships are a little more complicated. So, if you're not in a romantic relationship but are looking for one, find someone with a similar outlook on life. You can even discuss your targets with a person you might begin a serious relationship with. If you're planning to get married, make sure you are both on the same page for the life you want to create together. I would also highly recommend premarital counseling before you get married. Sometimes feelings at the beginning of relationships can cause people to overlook things that will become issues later on. If you are in a committed relationship, take some time to reflect on it. If you notice some negative areas, it doesn't necessarily mean you should end it. It does mean the areas need to be addressed. It might be as simple as an honest conversation, or it could require couples therapy. Just be honest with yourself here and remember a person you're in a romantic relationship with should be trustworthy and make you feel loved, appreciated, and respected. Sometimes, it is time to move on. Ending a relationship isn't easy, but don't waste years of your life with the wrong person to avoid the short term pain of ending a relationship you know deep down cannot be saved.

If you are in an abusive relationship, whether it be emotional, verbal, or physical, know that absolutely no one deserves abuse. As scary as it is, there is help. You may feel your situation is hopeless or there is no way out, but there is. It is hard to go through breaking free from an abusive relationship alone. Getting support can help you find the way out. Please reach out to an organization such as The National Domestic Violence Hotline by phone at 800-799-7233 or online at https://www.thehotline.org or Help Guide's domestic violence section online at https://www.helpguide.org if you find yourself in an abusive situation.

Take some time to reflect on the relationships in your life.

Who brings positivity into your life?

_____
_____
_____
_____
_____
_____
_____
_____

Who brings negativity into your life?

Which relationships do you want to nurture?

Which relationships have some things that need to be addressed? How can you address those issues?

Which relationships need to end? Do you need help ending any relationships? Where can you get help and support?

Would you like to foster new relationships? What are some ways you might do that?

How can you love and show those in your life you appreciate them?

Joy Target

It's time to set your target to fill your life with joy! Review your revised list at the beginning of this chapter, the images you found, and any other thoughts and ideas that have come up to help you reflect and then set your target below.

Again, gather your thoughts below and break the path to your joy target into small, simple steps to get you there.

72

Taking Aim with Actions

Continuing with your spirit, health, and presentation practices, add your joy practices along with small steps toward your targets.

Schedule in…

- Your giving activity
- Your random act of kindness
- Your spiritual practice
- Your forgiveness check (Do you need to forgive yourself or anyone else?)
- Your cardio, strength, and stretching/flexibility exercises for each week
- Any stressors or "hang-ups" to be addressed
- Passion/hobby
- Evaluate and plan steps to improve your spaces
- Evaluate and plan steps to create, improve, or end relationships

---

Pick at least 1 step toward your target for each element & schedule…

Spirit:_____

Health:_____

Presentation:_____

Joy:_____

Joy

	Sunday	Monday	Tuesday	Wednesday	Thursday	Friday	Saturday	*Reward*
Week 1	__ AM, Noon, & PM: Close your eyes, picture presence image, and take 3 slow, deep breaths __ Stay hydrated __ Presence activity/stress release activity __ Gratitude journal __ To sleep at bedtime *Healthy food swap for the week:* *Healthy recipe to try this week:*	__ AM, Noon, & PM: Close your eyes, picture presence image, and take 3 slow, deep breaths __ Stay hydrated __ Presence activity/stress release activity __ Gratitude journal __ To sleep at bedtime	__ AM, Noon, & PM: Close your eyes, picture presence image, and take 3 slow, deep breaths __ Stay hydrated __ Presence activity/stress release activity __ Gratitude journal __ To sleep at bedtime	__ AM, Noon, & PM: Close your eyes, picture presence image, and take 3 slow, deep breaths __ Stay hydrated __ Presence activity/stress release activity __ Gratitude journal __ To sleep at bedtime	__ AM, Noon, & PM: Close your eyes, picture presence image, and take 3 slow, deep breaths __ Stay hydrated __ Presence activity/stress release activity __ Gratitude journal __ To sleep at bedtime	__ AM, Noon, & PM: Close your eyes, picture presence image, and take 3 slow, deep breaths __ Stay hydrated __ Presence activity/stress release activity __ Gratitude journal __ To sleep at bedtime	__ AM, Noon, & PM: Close your eyes, picture presence image, and take 3 slow, deep breaths __ Stay hydrated __ Presence activity/stress release activity __ Gratitude journal __ To sleep at bedtime	
Week 2	__ AM, Noon, & PM: Close your eyes, picture presence image, and take 3 slow, deep breaths __ Stay hydrated __ Presence activity/stress release activity __ Gratitude journal __ To sleep at bedtime *Healthy food swap for the week:* *Healthy recipe to try this week:*	__ AM, Noon, & PM: Close your eyes, picture presence image, and take 3 slow, deep breaths __ Stay hydrated __ Presence activity/stress release activity __ Gratitude journal __ To sleep at bedtime	__ AM, Noon, & PM: Close your eyes, picture presence image, and take 3 slow, deep breaths __ Stay hydrated __ Presence activity/stress release activity __ Gratitude journal __ To sleep at bedtime	__ AM, Noon, & PM: Close your eyes, picture presence image, and take 3 slow, deep breaths __ Stay hydrated __ Presence activity/stress release activity __ Gratitude journal __ To sleep at bedtime	__ AM, Noon, & PM: Close your eyes, picture presence image, and take 3 slow, deep breaths __ Stay hydrated __ Presence activity/stress release activity __ Gratitude journal __ To sleep at bedtime	__ AM, Noon, & PM: Close your eyes, picture presence image, and take 3 slow, deep breaths __ Stay hydrated __ Presence activity/stress release activity __ Gratitude journal __ To sleep at bedtime	__ AM, Noon, & PM: Close your eyes, picture presence image, and take 3 slow, deep breaths __ Stay hydrated __ Presence activity/stress release activity __ Gratitude journal __ To sleep at bedtime	

Daily Spirit Reminders…

- Focus on the positive
- Express gratitude
- Shift your perspective on obligations as an opportunity to give

Daily Health Reminders…

- Eat real, unprocessed food
- Finish eating 3 to 4 hours before bed
- Go 12 to 14 hours between last and first meal

Joy

Joy

	Sunday	Monday	Tuesday	Wednesday	Thursday	Friday	Saturday	Reward
Week 3	__ AM, Noon, & PM: Close your eyes, picture presence image, and take 3 slow, deep breaths __ Stay hydrated __ Presence activity/stress release activity __ Gratitude journal __ To sleep at bedtime *Healthy food swap for the week: *Healthy recipe to try this week:	__ AM, Noon, & PM: Close your eyes, picture presence image, and take 3 slow, deep breaths __ Stay hydrated __ Presence activity/stress release activity __ Gratitude journal __ To sleep at bedtime	__ AM, Noon, & PM: Close your eyes, picture presence image, and take 3 slow, deep breaths __ Stay hydrated __ Presence activity/stress release activity __ Gratitude journal __ To sleep at bedtime	__ AM, Noon, & PM: Close your eyes, picture presence image, and take 3 slow, deep breaths __ Stay hydrated __ Presence activity/stress release activity __ Gratitude journal __ To sleep at bedtime	__ AM, Noon, & PM: Close your eyes, picture presence image, and take 3 slow, deep breaths __ Stay hydrated __ Presence activity/stress release activity __ Gratitude journal __ To sleep at bedtime	__ AM, Noon, & PM: Close your eyes, picture presence image, and take 3 slow, deep breaths __ Stay hydrated __ Presence activity/stress release activity __ Gratitude journal __ To sleep at bedtime	__ AM, Noon, & PM: Close your eyes, picture presence image, and take 3 slow, deep breaths __ Stay hydrated __ Presence activity/stress release activity __ Gratitude journal __ To sleep at bedtime	🎁
Week 4	__ AM, Noon, & PM: Close your eyes, picture presence image, and take 3 slow, deep breaths __ Stay hydrated __ Presence activity/stress release activity __ Gratitude journal __ To sleep at bedtime *Healthy food swap for the week: *Healthy recipe to try this week:	__ AM, Noon, & PM: Close your eyes, picture presence image, and take 3 slow, deep breaths __ Stay hydrated __ Presence activity/stress release activity __ Gratitude journal __ To sleep at bedtime	__ AM, Noon, & PM: Close your eyes, picture presence image, and take 3 slow, deep breaths __ Stay hydrated __ Presence activity/stress release activity __ Gratitude journal __ To sleep at bedtime	__ AM, Noon, & PM: Close your eyes, picture presence image, and take 3 slow, deep breaths __ Stay hydrated __ Presence activity/stress release activity __ Gratitude journal __ To sleep at bedtime	__ AM, Noon, & PM: Close your eyes, picture presence image, and take 3 slow, deep breaths __ Stay hydrated __ Presence activity/stress release activity __ Gratitude journal __ To sleep at bedtime	__ AM, Noon, & PM: Close your eyes, picture presence image, and take 3 slow, deep breaths __ Stay hydrated __ Presence activity/stress release activity __ Gratitude journal __ To sleep at bedtime	__ AM, Noon, & PM: Close your eyes, picture presence image, and take 3 slow, deep breaths __ Stay hydrated __ Presence activity/stress release activity __ Gratitude journal __ To sleep at bedtime	🎁

Daily Presentation Reminders…
- Keep up with grooming practices
- Stance check-ins

Daily Joy Reminders…
- Focus on the good and sprinkle joy throughout each day
- Nurture positive relationships
- Express love & appreciation

ORGANIZATION

For some people the element of organization comes easily. For others, not so much. This is an element you have to make work for you. It will look different for different people. Some may take it further than others, but having order in your life is important. As we go through this element, remember that things will get dirty, out of order, and off schedule. My intention in this element is to set you up to keep on top of life's demands, not turn you into a perfectionist.

Organization takes some effort up front, but it makes life easier in the long run. This chapter will focus on decluttering, cleaning, arranging, keeping up with your obligations, scheduling, and money. I hope it helps your life flow and works for you. As you go through this chapter, take my suggestions as examples to get you thinking and modify them in ways that make sense to you. It's time to begin by listing how you feel you're off track in the element of organization. Then replace that with the opposite.

_____
_____
_____
_____
_____
_____
_____
_____
_____
_____

Spaces

Let's start with physical spaces (i.e. your home, room, yard, porch, automobile, office, or even your purse/wallet). We touched on this in the joy chapter, but I want you to look at your spaces again through the element of organization.

I wish I could wave a magic wand and do this for you, but you're going to have to put in some work here. It will be worth it though. First, list your physical spaces below.

Next, I want you to declutter them. One by one go through each space and give away, sell, recycle, or throw out everything you don't like or use. If it's broken, and you know you're not going to fix it, get rid of it. If it reminds you of something unpleasant, get rid of it. The key is to purge here. Check off each space after you've finished decluttering them.

Once you've removed the clutter, I want you to organize each space in a way that works for you. Filing systems, baskets, storage areas, containers, and labels are helpful with this. Make sure everything has a place that's easily accessible as needed. Again, check off the space once it's organized.

Finally give each space a good cleaning and check off each space after it's cleaned.

Space	Decluttered	Organized	Cleaned
_____	___	___	___
_____	___	___	___
_____	___	___	___
_____	___	___	___
_____	___	___	___
_____	___	___	___
_____	___	___	___

I also wish once a space was decluttered, organized, and cleaned it would stay that way, but that's not the way things are. Set aside time each day to take the actions needed to keep items from piling up and cluttering your spaces and commit to keeping them organized and clean. When something comes into your space, put it where it goes. If you don't like or don't want it, don't bring it in. Remember things such as mail or email. When paperwork like mail or email piles up, it creates clutter and stress.

Obligations

In life we have many obligations. It makes things easier if you can find a way to keep track of and organize them. Let's start by listing the recurring obligations you have in your life. Here are some things to get you thinking… Do you have yearly appointments such as doctor and dentist visits or vet checkups for your pets? Do you have birthdays for friends and family to remember? Do you have certifications you need to renew?

My recurring obligations

_____   _____
_____   _____
_____   _____
_____   _____
_____   _____

Now decide if you'd like to use pen and paper or go digital to organize your obligations.

For your recurring obligations, I recommend some sort of master list you can refer to as you're planning out your year.

Schedule

Life gets busy, and it's important to find a way to organize your schedule. Again, decide if you prefer pen and paper or going digital.

I suggest having a big picture, yearly calendar to schedule upcoming events, appointments, or reminders you might need to note for the year to come. Refer to your master list from the obligations section and schedule appointments, birthdays, renewals, holidays, vacations, etc.

I also suggest monthly calendars. You can start by referring to your yearly calendar as you start each month and note anything already scheduled. Then you can zoom into what goals you'd like to accomplish and add any other activities or events needed for the month.

From there I find it helpful to have a daily schedule. There you can add more specific tasks, along with goals and priorities and anything else that pops up.

I've given a very basic, quick example below of each to give you some ideas to fine tune and create your scheduling system.

Big Picture…

January	February	March	April
Yearly physical	6 Month dental visit		Vacation (5th-15th)

May	June	July	August
Pup's vet checkup			6 Month dental visit

September	October	November	December
Jane's birthday September 7th		Renew certification	New Year's Eve party

Monthly…

February

Sun.	Mon.	Tues.	Wed.	Thurs.	Fri.	Sat.
1	2	3 Dentist at 2:00	4	5	6	7 Volunteer 11-12
8	9 Haircut at 4:30	10	11	12	13	14 Valentine's dinner
15	16	17	18	19	20 Book club at 7:30	21 Volunteer 11-12
22 Hike with Luke	23	24	25	26	27	28 Volunteer 11-12

Daily…

February 3rd

Meditate
Run with Sandra
Meeting with team to discus project
Dentist at 2
Grocery
Work in garden
Call Mom

Money

I am by no means an expert in finances, but I will discuss some fundamental principles.

The first principle is to live within your means. This is hard in our society with credit being the norm. Yet, I would highly recommend reviewing how much money you are bringing in, how much you pay in monthly bills, and how much money you have left. Take this and create a budget. Then avoid debt. It is a slippery slope. Other than a car, a home, and possibly school tuition, if there is something you would like that you don't have enough money for, save up for it. You don't know what the future holds, and if you already can't afford something and emergency costs come up, it makes it harder to pay off the debt you owe and creates the conditions to have to add more debt to your life. Sometimes emergencies, etc. come up that leave you little choice but to go into debt, or perhaps you find yourself already in debt. Make paying off that debt a priority.

The second principal is to save. Once you are debt free, minus a car, house, or student loans (make paying these off a priority along with saving), I suggest saving for your retirement, for an emergency fund, and finally for fun, goals, travel, etc.

The third principal is to make sure you have insurance (health, automobile, and home or rental) and that your will and affairs are in order.

The fourth principal I have to offer is to monitor your money. It's important to keep track of all your finances. You want to understand all of your accounts and make sure your money is in the best place. It might be worthwhile to check out some financial books at the library or listen to some podcasts on finances.

As a bonus principal, be generous with your money and help others in ways you are able. You can give to a charity that resonates with you, buy a homeless person a meal, or help out someone who is in need. I'll give an example of something someone did for me in my life. I had a cat with a tumor on her leg. She needed surgery to have it removed. The cost of the surgery was a strain at the time. When I went to pick her up, I was ready to put the cost on my credit card and was told someone had come in and paid for the surgery already. Talk about feeling gratitude!

Organization Target

It's time to set your target for organization below.

And now it's time for plotting the steps toward your organization target.

Taking Aim with Actions

Depending where you are starting from in the area of organization, this is an element where you might need to give yourself more than one month. If needed, there will be two calendars for this element. Another option might be to take away the pressure of having your spaces, obligations, schedule, and money organized all at once and incorporate these tasks as steps toward your target like the example below.

-> List spaces to organize (If the space has many areas, such as your home, break it up into smaller steps area by area.)
-> Declutter each space
-> Organize each space
-> Clean each space
-> Create a master list for your recurring obligations
-> Find a calendar system that works for you
-> Organize/plan your year
-> Organize/plan your month
-> Begin planning out your weeks and days
-> Create a budget
-> Create a plan to become debt free if applicable
-> Create a savings plan
-> Review/set up your insurance plans, will, and affairs
-> Schedule in monitoring and learning about money as needed
-> Find a way to be generous with money

Keep going with your spirit, health, presentation, and joy practices and add your organization practices along with small steps toward your targets.

Schedule in…

- Your giving activity
- Your random act of kindness
- Your spiritual practice
- Your forgiveness check (Do you need to forgive yourself or anyone else?)
- Your cardio, strength, and stretching/flexibility exercises for each week
- Any stressors or "hang-ups" to be addressed
- Passion/hobby
- Steps to organize your spaces, obligations, schedule, and money

---

Pick at least 1 step toward your target for each element & schedule…

Spirit:_____

Health:_____

Presentation:_____

Joy:_____

Organization:_____

Organization

	Sunday	Monday	Tuesday	Wednesday	Thursday	Friday	Saturday	*Reward*
Week 1	__ AM, Noon, & PM: Close your eyes, picture presence image, and take 3 slow, deep breaths __ Stay hydrated __ Presence activity/stress release activity __ Gratitude journal __ To sleep at bedtime *Healthy food swap for the week:* *Healthy recipe to try this week:*	__ AM, Noon, & PM: Close your eyes, picture presence image, and take 3 slow, deep breaths __ Stay hydrated __ Presence activity/stress release activity __ Gratitude journal __ To sleep at bedtime	__ AM, Noon, & PM: Close your eyes, picture presence image, and take 3 slow, deep breaths __ Stay hydrated __ Presence activity/stress release activity __ Gratitude journal __ To sleep at bedtime	__ AM, Noon, & PM: Close your eyes, picture presence image, and take 3 slow, deep breaths __ Stay hydrated __ Presence activity/stress release activity __ Gratitude journal __ To sleep at bedtime	__ AM, Noon, & PM: Close your eyes, picture presence image, and take 3 slow, deep breaths __ Stay hydrated __ Presence activity/stress release activity __ Gratitude journal __ To sleep at bedtime	__ AM, Noon, & PM: Close your eyes, picture presence image, and take 3 slow, deep breaths __ Stay hydrated __ Presence activity/stress release activity __ Gratitude journal __ To sleep at bedtime	__ AM, Noon, & PM: Close your eyes, picture presence image, and take 3 slow, deep breaths __ Stay hydrated __ Presence activity/stress release activity __ Gratitude journal __ To sleep at bedtime	🎁
Week 2	__ AM, Noon, & PM: Close your eyes, picture presence image, and take 3 slow, deep breaths __ Stay hydrated __ Presence activity/stress release activity __ Gratitude journal __ To sleep at bedtime *Healthy food swap for the week:* *Healthy recipe to try this week:*	__ AM, Noon, & PM: Close your eyes, picture presence image, and take 3 slow, deep breaths __ Stay hydrated __ Presence activity/stress release activity __ Gratitude journal __ To sleep at bedtime	__ AM, Noon, & PM: Close your eyes, picture presence image, and take 3 slow, deep breaths __ Stay hydrated __ Presence activity/stress release activity __ Gratitude journal __ To sleep at bedtime	__ AM, Noon, & PM: Close your eyes, picture presence image, and take 3 slow, deep breaths __ Stay hydrated __ Presence activity/stress release activity __ Gratitude journal __ To sleep at bedtime	__ AM, Noon, & PM: Close your eyes, picture presence image, and take 3 slow, deep breaths __ Stay hydrated __ Presence activity/stress release activity __ Gratitude journal __ To sleep at bedtime	__ AM, Noon, & PM: Close your eyes, picture presence image, and take 3 slow, deep breaths __ Stay hydrated __ Presence activity/stress release activity __ Gratitude journal __ To sleep at bedtime	__ AM, Noon, & PM: Close your eyes, picture presence image, and take 3 slow, deep breaths __ Stay hydrated __ Presence activity/stress release activity __ Gratitude journal __ To sleep at bedtime	🎁

Daily Spirit Reminders...
- Focus on the positive
- Express gratitude
- Shift your perspective on obligations as an opportunity to give

Daily Health Reminders...
- Eat real, unprocessed food
- Finish eating 3 to 4 hours before bed
- Go 12 to 14 hours between last and first meal

Daily Presentation Reminders...
- Keep up with grooming practices
- Stance check-ins

Organization

	Sunday	Monday	Tuesday	Wednesday	Thursday	Friday	Saturday	*Reward*
Week 3	__ AM, Noon, & PM: Close your eyes, picture presence image, and take 3 slow, deep breaths __ Stay hydrated __ Presence activity/stress release activity __ Gratitude journal __ To sleep at bedtime *Healthy food swap for the week* *Healthy recipe to try this week*	__ AM, Noon, & PM: Close your eyes, picture presence image, and take 3 slow, deep breaths __ Stay hydrated __ Presence activity/stress release activity __ Gratitude journal __ To sleep at bedtime	__ AM, Noon, & PM: Close your eyes, picture presence image, and take 3 slow, deep breaths __ Stay hydrated __ Presence activity/stress release activity __ Gratitude journal __ To sleep at bedtime	__ AM, Noon, & PM: Close your eyes, picture presence image, and take 3 slow, deep breaths __ Stay hydrated __ Presence activity/stress release activity __ Gratitude journal __ To sleep at bedtime	__ AM, Noon, & PM: Close your eyes, picture presence image, and take 3 slow, deep breaths __ Stay hydrated __ Presence activity/stress release activity __ Gratitude journal __ To sleep at bedtime	__ AM, Noon, & PM: Close your eyes, picture presence image, and take 3 slow, deep breaths __ Stay hydrated __ Presence activity/stress release activity __ Gratitude journal __ To sleep at bedtime	__ AM, Noon, & PM: Close your eyes, picture presence image, and take 3 slow, deep breaths __ Stay hydrated __ Presence activity/stress release activity __ Gratitude journal __ To sleep at bedtime	🎁
Week 4	__ AM, Noon, & PM: Close your eyes, picture presence image, and take 3 slow, deep breaths __ Stay hydrated __ Presence activity/stress release activity __ Gratitude journal __ To sleep at bedtime *Healthy food swap for the week* *Healthy recipe to try this week*	__ AM, Noon, & PM: Close your eyes, picture presence image, and take 3 slow, deep breaths __ Stay hydrated __ Presence activity/stress release activity __ Gratitude journal __ To sleep at bedtime	__ AM, Noon, & PM: Close your eyes, picture presence image, and take 3 slow, deep breaths __ Stay hydrated __ Presence activity/stress release activity __ Gratitude journal __ To sleep at bedtime	__ AM, Noon, & PM: Close your eyes, picture presence image, and take 3 slow, deep breaths __ Stay hydrated __ Presence activity/stress release activity __ Gratitude journal __ To sleep at bedtime	__ AM, Noon, & PM: Close your eyes, picture presence image, and take 3 slow, deep breaths __ Stay hydrated __ Presence activity/stress release activity __ Gratitude journal __ To sleep at bedtime	__ AM, Noon, & PM: Close your eyes, picture presence image, and take 3 slow, deep breaths __ Stay hydrated __ Presence activity/stress release activity __ Gratitude journal __ To sleep at bedtime	__ AM, Noon, & PM: Close your eyes, picture presence image, and take 3 slow, deep breaths __ Stay hydrated __ Presence activity/stress release activity __ Gratitude journal __ To sleep at bedtime	🎁

Daily Joy Reminders...
- Focus on the good and sprinkle joy throughout each day
- Nurture positive relationships
- Express love and appreciation

Daily Organization Reminders...
- Set aside time each day to keep organized and clean

Organization

	Sunday	Monday	Tuesday	Wednesday	Thursday	Friday	Saturday	Reward
Week 5	__ AM, Noon, & PM: Close your eyes, picture presence image, and take 3 slow, deep breaths __ Stay hydrated __ Presence activity/stress release activity __ Gratitude journal __ To sleep at bedtime *Healthy food swap for the week: *Healthy recipe to try this week:	__ AM, Noon, & PM: Close your eyes, picture presence image, and take 3 slow, deep breaths __ Stay hydrated __ Presence activity/stress release activity __ Gratitude journal __ To sleep at bedtime	__ AM, Noon, & PM: Close your eyes, picture presence image, and take 3 slow, deep breaths __ Stay hydrated __ Presence activity/stress release activity __ Gratitude journal __ To sleep at bedtime	__ AM, Noon, & PM: Close your eyes, picture presence image, and take 3 slow, deep breaths __ Stay hydrated __ Presence activity/stress release activity __ Gratitude journal __ To sleep at bedtime	__ AM, Noon, & PM: Close your eyes, picture presence image, and take 3 slow, deep breaths __ Stay hydrated __ Presence activity/stress release activity __ Gratitude journal __ To sleep at bedtime	__ AM, Noon, & PM: Close your eyes, picture presence image, and take 3 slow, deep breaths __ Stay hydrated __ Presence activity/stress release activity __ Gratitude journal __ To sleep at bedtime	__ AM, Noon, & PM: Close your eyes, picture presence image, and take 3 slow, deep breaths __ Stay hydrated __ Presence activity/stress release activity __ Gratitude journal __ To sleep at bedtime	
Week 6	__ AM, Noon, & PM: Close your eyes, picture presence image, and take 3 slow, deep breaths __ Stay hydrated __ Presence activity/stress release activity __ Gratitude journal __ To sleep at bedtime *Healthy food swap for the week: *Healthy recipe to try this week:	__ AM, Noon, & PM: Close your eyes, picture presence image, and take 3 slow, deep breaths __ Stay hydrated __ Presence activity/stress release activity __ Gratitude journal __ To sleep at bedtime	__ AM, Noon, & PM: Close your eyes, picture presence image, and take 3 slow, deep breaths __ Stay hydrated __ Presence activity/stress release activity __ Gratitude journal __ To sleep at bedtime	__ AM, Noon, & PM: Close your eyes, picture presence image, and take 3 slow, deep breaths __ Stay hydrated __ Presence activity/stress release activity __ Gratitude journal __ To sleep at bedtime	__ AM, Noon, & PM: Close your eyes, picture presence image, and take 3 slow, deep breaths __ Stay hydrated __ Presence activity/stress release activity __ Gratitude journal __ To sleep at bedtime	__ AM, Noon, & PM: Close your eyes, picture presence image, and take 3 slow, deep breaths __ Stay hydrated __ Presence activity/stress release activity __ Gratitude journal __ To sleep at bedtime	__ AM, Noon, & PM: Close your eyes, picture presence image, and take 3 slow, deep breaths __ Stay hydrated __ Presence activity/stress release activity __ Gratitude journal __ To sleep at bedtime	

Daily Spirit Reminders…

- Focus on the positive
- Express gratitude
- Shift your perspective on obligations as an opportunity to give

Daily Health Reminders…

- Eat real, unprocessed food
- Finish eating 3 to 4 hours before bed
- Go 12 to 14 hours between last and first meal

Daily Presentation Reminders…

- Keep up with grooming practices
- Stance check-ins

Organization

	Sunday	Monday	Tuesday	Wednesday	Thursday	Friday	Saturday	*Reward*
Week 7	__ AM, Noon, & PM: Close your eyes, picture presence image, and take 3 slow, deep breaths __ Stay hydrated __ Presence activity/stress release activity __ Gratitude journal __ To sleep at bedtime *Healthy food swap for the week:* *Healthy recipe to try this week:*	__ AM, Noon, & PM: Close your eyes, picture presence image, and take 3 slow, deep breaths __ Stay hydrated __ Presence activity/stress release activity __ Gratitude journal __ To sleep at bedtime	__ AM, Noon, & PM: Close your eyes, picture presence image, and take 3 slow, deep breaths __ Stay hydrated __ Presence activity/stress release activity __ Gratitude journal __ To sleep at bedtime	__ AM, Noon, & PM: Close your eyes, picture presence image, and take 3 slow, deep breaths __ Stay hydrated __ Presence activity/stress release activity __ Gratitude journal __ To sleep at bedtime	__ AM, Noon, & PM: Close your eyes, picture presence image, and take 3 slow, deep breaths __ Stay hydrated __ Presence activity/stress release activity __ Gratitude journal __ To sleep at bedtime	__ AM, Noon, & PM: Close your eyes, picture presence image, and take 3 slow, deep breaths __ Stay hydrated __ Presence activity/stress release activity __ Gratitude journal __ To sleep at bedtime	__ AM, Noon, & PM: Close your eyes, picture presence image, and take 3 slow, deep breaths __ Stay hydrated __ Presence activity/stress release activity __ Gratitude journal __ To sleep at bedtime	
Week 8	__ AM, Noon, & PM: Close your eyes, picture presence image, and take 3 slow, deep breaths __ Stay hydrated __ Presence activity/stress release activity __ Gratitude journal __ To sleep at bedtime *Healthy food swap for the week:* *Healthy recipe to try this week:*	__ AM, Noon, & PM: Close your eyes, picture presence image, and take 3 slow, deep breaths __ Stay hydrated __ Presence activity/stress release activity __ Gratitude journal __ To sleep at bedtime	__ AM, Noon, & PM: Close your eyes, picture presence image, and take 3 slow, deep breaths __ Stay hydrated __ Presence activity/stress release activity __ Gratitude journal __ To sleep at bedtime	__ AM, Noon, & PM: Close your eyes, picture presence image, and take 3 slow, deep breaths __ Stay hydrated __ Presence activity/stress release activity __ Gratitude journal __ To sleep at bedtime	__ AM, Noon, & PM: Close your eyes, picture presence image, and take 3 slow, deep breaths __ Stay hydrated __ Presence activity/stress release activity __ Gratitude journal __ To sleep at bedtime	__ AM, Noon, & PM: Close your eyes, picture presence image, and take 3 slow, deep breaths __ Stay hydrated __ Presence activity/stress release activity __ Gratitude journal __ To sleep at bedtime	__ AM, Noon, & PM: Close your eyes, picture presence image, and take 3 slow, deep breaths __ Stay hydrated __ Presence activity/stress release activity __ Gratitude journal __ To sleep at bedtime	

Daily Joy Reminders…
- Focus on the good and sprinkle joy throughout each day
- Nurture positive relationships
- Express love and appreciation

Daily Organization Reminders…
- Set aside time each day to keep organized and clean

YOUR FUTURE

It's time to dream big in this chapter. What do you want your future to be? The way to the future you want is to get clear about what it is you want. As you're thinking about and designing your future, check in and make sure your dreams are yours, not what friends, loved ones, or society has told you that you should want or that you're limited to. Unfortunately, most people have been told in one way or another what their limits are, what career path they should take, or what success is, etc. To begin this chapter, I'm going to change up the exercise we've been doing. You can't list where you feel your future is off since it hasn't happened yet. Instead, I want you to list the limits you feel or have been told your future has.

Next, write the opposite of those limits and post it over them. For example, if you think you won't have enough money, replace that with more than enough money. Within the parameters of reason, which can be stretched more than we sometimes realize, the truth is your future is only limited to what you can dream of and are willing to work toward. Don't limit yourself to others' status quos and society's norms. You can make your grandest dreams come true! The possibilities are up to you!

Place/Places

The area in which you live can have a big impact on you. I think many people just live in a place without much thought or think they will move to their dream location once they retire. If you already live in your dream location, that's great. If not, this section is for you. I propose for you to get very clear on where you'd like to live and begin taking steps to get yourself there now. You may not be able to move overnight if you find you're not in your dream location, but getting clear about your target will allow you to take aim and take the steps to get you there sooner rather than later. Ask yourself the following questions and journal your way to your perfect location or locations below. Don't let worries about how get in the way of what you desire. Just write your feelings from your heart with no limits.

Where would you love to live? Would you prefer a big bustling city, the suburbs, or a remote location? What do you want to be surrounded by? Do you want to be near the ocean, a river, or a lake? Do you want to be in the mountains, a forest, or a desert? Do you prefer tropical weather or snow? Is there a foreign country where you've dreamed of living? Is there a place where you want to live and never move, or would you love to move around and experience a variety of places throughout your life?

_____
_____
_____
_____
_____
_____
_____
_____
_____
_____
_____
_____
_____
_____
_____
_____
_____
_____
_____
_____
_____
_____
_____
_____
_____
_____
_____
_____

I will assume you aren't able to pack up and move tomorrow (of course, if you can, go for it), so let's start by listing steps to get "your arrow" moving toward your target. If you want to live in multiple places, list them in the order you think will work best for you. If you are in your college years, attend a school in an area you love. If you want to live in a foreign country, start taking lessons in the country's language. Surround yourself with some images of or objects from the place or places you'd like to live. Research the area or areas. Apply to jobs in that location. Take some trips there. Look at real-estate there. Below list some steps to get you headed in the direction toward the place(s) you'd love to live. Take one step at a time and keep going until you get where you want to be.

_____
_____
_____
_____
_____
_____
_____
_____
_____
_____
_____
_____
_____
_____
_____
_____
_____

Home

I believe your home should be a place to comfort you, recharge you, lift your spirits, and inspire you. It should be a retreat from the world where you're surrounded by sights, smells, sounds, textures, and tastes that reflect you and you enjoy. Get back into the space of not worrying about the how and just thinking about what you'd love. Collect some images from architectural and decorating magazines of what you'd love your home to be like and glue them on a poster or collect some images digitally. Reflecting on what you've picked, fill out the questions below to know what you'd like to be surrounded by in your home.

What is your style? (Do you like modern, rustic, vintage, antique, farmhouse, eclectic, or minimalist? Do you prefer a formal or causal space? Do you want a big or small space? Would you prefer to live on a large piece of land, a zero lot line home, or an apartment in a high-rise?)

_____
_____
_____
_____
_____
_____
_____
_____
_____
_____
_____
_____

What do you want to see in your home? (What colors would you love? What patterns do you like? What type of lighting do you want? Do you want big windows with sun coming in or cozy drapes, lamps, and dimmers? How can you display your interests, goals, important pictures, and fond memories? Would you like plants or flowers in vases? Would you like to display collections?)

Think about your sense of touch. What textures do you prefer? What do you want to feel in your home? (What fabrics would you like for your furniture? What would you like your bedding and blankets to feel like? Would you like to change things for fall, winter, spring, and/or summer? What would you like to feel under your feet—rugs, tile, wood, or carpet? How would you like to make the temperature comfortable—fireplaces, fire pits, heated floors in the bathrooms, windows open with screens, or fans?)

What smells would you like your home to be filled with? (Would you like fragrant flowers such as jasmine by your front door to inhale as you enter? Would you enjoy some potted herbs in your kitchen such as lavender and rosemary? Do you want screens so you can open the windows to let in fresh air? What aromas can you imagine filling your home as you're cooking?)

_____
_____
_____
_____
_____
_____
_____
_____
_____
_____
_____
_____
_____
_____
_____
_____
_____
_____
_____
_____
_____
_____
_____
_____
_____
_____
_____
_____

How would you like to nurture your sense of taste in your home? (Would you like to put fruit in bowls? How would you like to organize healthy food to make it easily available? Do you want to store dried goods such as beans and legumes in beautiful glass jars? Would you like a big garden or some potted herbs and tomatoes?)

_____
_____
_____
_____

What sounds would you like to hear in your home? (Do you want instruments displayed for playing? How about a nice stereo system? Would you like to hear birds chirping, chimes ringing, or dogs barking? Do you want your home to be a quiet retreat or filled with laughter and conversation?)

You may not be able to move into your dream home tomorrow, but you can begin taking steps toward it, such as saving up for a down payment. In the meantime, whether you live in a room in someone else's home, a dorm, an apartment, a rental, or a starter home you can begin filling it with the ideas you've listed above.

Career

There are exceptions, but most people have to work in order to earn money. Whether you're just beginning college, applying for your first job, or have been in a career for some time, it's important to evaluate and choose what you would like to do. Your work and career take up a lot of your time on this earth. I believe it's important to find something you feel passionate about and enjoy and to surround yourself with positive people. It may not be perfect at all times (nothing is), but if it drains your spirit, that impacts your life negatively. If you're just beginning, choose carefully. If you're already working, evaluate carefully. If your job is making you unhappy, stressed, or uninspired, you have the power to change that. It's never too late to change. You may have found the career that's right for you already. If so, that's wonderful. Keep at it. If you're trying to choose a career or feel you need a change, answer the following questions to get you aimed toward a career that's right for you.

What did you want to be when you were younger?

What are you passionate about?

What do you enjoy learning?

What are your talents?

Do you feel like people in your life, such as your parents, have set expectations about your career path? Is it a career path you want?

What are some jobs that incorporate your passions and talents?

Would you prefer to work for a company or person, or would you prefer to be your own boss?

If you could snap your fingers and have any job in the world tomorrow with all the school, training, interviews, etc. behind you, what would your dream job be?

Okay, reflect on your answers above. If you still aren't clear, try finding your Ikigai. Ikigai is a Japanese concept to help guide you toward uniting what you love and are good at with the world's needs. Start by listing what you love, what you're good at, and what the world needs and reflect on anything that overlaps and you can earn a living in. When you're ready, list some jobs/careers you feel are calling you. Then look into what type of school or training you need to attain them. Career counselors might be a good resource or talk to some people already working in a field you're interested in. If you are already in a career and want to make a shift, it may seem very overwhelming and feel like it may take too long. Even so, my dad once gave me the following advice. Whatever amount of time it will take to get you to the career you want will pass either way. When that time has passed, you can still be stuck in a job you dread going to or be prepared to make the change to one you're meant for. In other words, those years will pass either way, and after the time has passed, you can be stuck in the same place or moving to where you want to be. Granted it may take some hard work and sacrifices, but if you really want it, it's worth it. As long as you're still on the earth, it's never too late.

In the mean time, put your best effort forward in whatever you are doing. Aim for excellence, and it will be noticed. I love the quote by Dr. Martin Luther King Jr. "If a man is called to be a street sweeper, he should sweep streets even as Michelangelo painted, or Beethoven composed music, or Shakespeare wrote poetry. He should sweep streets so well that all the hosts of heaven and earth will push to say, `Here lived a great street sweeper who did his job well.`"

Reflections on career…

Family/Pets

You may already have a partner and six kids with a barn full of animals, or you may just be beginning to think about this. But, just like every aspect of your life, it's important to choose what works for you. I'm going to start off with some thoughts if you're the latter and just beginning to think about this. If you're already in full family swing, skip to the next section.

This is an area where society and people such as parents set expectations. So, I want you to take time and consider what you truly would like.

Do you want to get married? Do you want to have children? Would you prefer to adopt? How many kids would you like? Would you prefer to get married or have a partner in life but not have children? Does the single life appeal to you?

_____

In my view pets are part of the family, so would you like pets in your life? If so, what kind and how many? Will they stay outside or be curled up with you in bed at night?

_____

Now think about the feelings, relationships, and general atmosphere you want for your family. If you have children, do you want to stay home with them or have your spouse or partner stay home with them? Would you prefer to continue to work and hire a nanny or have them attend daycare? How will you all treat each other? What will your values be? What would you like to do together? If you would prefer to be single and not have children, think about how some of these questions may apply to any pets you will have or when friends and extended family visit. Remember these thoughts as you build your life. If you choose to get married or live with a partner, be sure to discuss this with that person and make sure you both want the same things.

If you already have built a family, take some time to reflect on the questions below.

Are you happy with your relationship with your spouse or partner? Are there ways you'd like to improve your relationship such as communication or spending more time together? Are there more serious issues that might need to be addressed through counseling?

Do you have children? Would you like to? Either way, would you like to have or adopt (more) children?

Do you have pets? Would you like one or more? What kinds?

Now think about the feelings, relationships, and general atmosphere in your family. How does everyone treat each other? Do you all live by your values? Are there areas you'd like to change or improve? If you have children, do you stay home with them or does your spouse or partner stay home with them? Do you work and hire a nanny or have your child or children attend daycare? Are you happy with that or would you prefer to change the arrangements? Does your family have fun together? What are some things you could add to make your family life more fun?

Your Future

Activities

Now I want you to create a list of activities you are interested in pursuing. Under each topic list some things you'd be interested in throughout your life.

Where would you like to travel in your life?

_____
_____
_____
_____
_____
_____
_____
_____
_____
_____
_____

What are some things you'd like to learn in your life?

_____
_____
_____
_____
_____
_____
_____
_____
_____
_____
_____

What are some hobbies and passions you'd like to pursue in your life?

_____
_____
_____
_____
_____
_____
_____
_____
_____
_____
_____
_____

What are some things you'd like to experience or try in your life?

_____
_____
_____
_____
_____
_____
_____
_____
_____
_____
_____
_____

You've probably heard the saying life is a marathon, not a sprint. Don't feel like you have to complete the above lists all at once. Think of the lists as inspirations that you can refer back to and pursue throughout your life. If you complete them all, make new lists and keep on having fun and enjoying your life!

Who

When thinking about your future, it's important to think about who you aim to be. As we come to the end this book, this brings us back full circle to spirit in a way. In my opinion, when you reflect on your life, it's not about how much money, power, or things you've acquired. Not that those things are bad in and of themselves, but they aren't what really matters or makes you who you are. It's about how you treat others, love, and contribute to this earth and all those we share it with. Choose and reflect often on who you want to be and make sure your thoughts and actions are reflecting that. The last questions will help you get clear about who you target to be.

Imagine you're at the end of your life. What will you be most proud of?

___

___

___

___

___

___

___

___

___

___

___

___

___

___

___

___

___

___

___

___

___

___

___

___

___

___

___

___

___

___

After you've passed, what do you want your friends and loved ones to remember about you?

How do you want to treat others and show love?

What would you like to contribute to this earth and those we share it with?

Who (think character, nature, disposition, and core self) do you aim to be?

What are daily actions you can take to be the person you want to be throughout your life?

Your Future

Future Target

You've arrived at the last target. As you set your future target, don't hold yourself back by your present circumstances. Allow your imagination and heart's desires to set a target for the future you truly want. Reflect on the work you've done and ideas you've had throughout this chapter to set a target for the future of you dreams.

◎
_____
_____
_____
_____
_____
_____
_____
_____
_____
_____
_____
_____
_____
_____
_____
_____
_____
_____
_____
_____
_____
_____
_____
_____
_____
_____
_____
_____
_____
_____

As you begin to map out the steps to your future target, it might seem daunting. If it's difficult to see a clear path, don't let that discourage you. Come up with some actionable steps that will provide you with knowledge about or experiences that relate to what you want or focus on one small aspect of your target at a time. Once you start taking actions, it is likely the next steps will follow naturally, and you'll be able to keep going. The key is to know what your target is and to keep moving toward it.

Target Your Life

Taking Aim with Actions

For the last action calendar, you will put all the elements together and add actions for your future target. Going forward you can continue to create calendars like this, or you can incorporate your habits and action steps in your own calendar system. Just remember to keep taking steps toward you targets.

Schedule in…

- Your giving activity
- Your random act of kindness
- Your spiritual practice
- Your forgiveness check (Do you need to forgive yourself or anyone else?)
- Your cardio, strength, and stretching/flexibility exercises for each week
- Any stressors or "hang-ups" to be addressed
- Passion/hobby

Pick at least 1 step toward your target for each element & schedule…

Spirit:_____

Health:_____

Presentation:_____

Joy:_____

Organization:_____

Your Future:_____

Your Future

	Sunday	Monday	Tuesday	Wednesday	Thursday	Friday	Saturday	*Reward*
Week 1	__ AM, Noon, & PM: Close your eyes, picture presence image, and take 3 slow, deep breaths __ Stay hydrated __ Presence activity/stress release activity __ Gratitude journal __ To sleep at bedtime *Healthy food swap for the week:* *Healthy recipe to try this week:*	__ AM, Noon, & PM: Close your eyes, picture presence image, and take 3 slow, deep breaths __ Stay hydrated __ Presence activity/stress release activity __ Gratitude journal __ To sleep at bedtime	__ AM, Noon, & PM: Close your eyes, picture presence image, and take 3 slow, deep breaths __ Stay hydrated __ Presence activity/stress release activity __ Gratitude journal __ To sleep at bedtime	__ AM, Noon, & PM: Close your eyes, picture presence image, and take 3 slow, deep breaths __ Stay hydrated __ Presence activity/stress release activity __ Gratitude journal __ To sleep at bedtime	__ AM, Noon, & PM: Close your eyes, picture presence image, and take 3 slow, deep breaths __ Stay hydrated __ Presence activity/stress release activity __ Gratitude journal __ To sleep at bedtime	__ AM, Noon, & PM: Close your eyes, picture presence image, and take 3 slow, deep breaths __ Stay hydrated __ Presence activity/stress release activity __ Gratitude journal __ To sleep at bedtime	__ AM, Noon, & PM: Close your eyes, picture presence image, and take 3 slow, deep breaths __ Stay hydrated __ Presence activity/stress release activity __ Gratitude journal __ To sleep at bedtime	
Week 2	__ AM, Noon, & PM: Close your eyes, picture presence image, and take 3 slow, deep breaths __ Stay hydrated __ Presence activity/stress release activity __ Gratitude journal __ To sleep at bedtime *Healthy food swap for the week:* *Healthy recipe to try this week:*	__ AM, Noon, & PM: Close your eyes, picture presence image, and take 3 slow, deep breaths __ Stay hydrated __ Presence activity/stress release activity __ Gratitude journal __ To sleep at bedtime	__ AM, Noon, & PM: Close your eyes, picture presence image, and take 3 slow, deep breaths __ Stay hydrated __ Presence activity/stress release activity __ Gratitude journal __ To sleep at bedtime	__ AM, Noon, & PM: Close your eyes, picture presence image, and take 3 slow, deep breaths __ Stay hydrated __ Presence activity/stress release activity __ Gratitude journal __ To sleep at bedtime	__ AM, Noon, & PM: Close your eyes, picture presence image, and take 3 slow, deep breaths __ Stay hydrated __ Presence activity/stress release activity __ Gratitude journal __ To sleep at bedtime	__ AM, Noon, & PM: Close your eyes, picture presence image, and take 3 slow, deep breaths __ Stay hydrated __ Presence activity/stress release activity __ Gratitude journal __ To sleep at bedtime	__ AM, Noon, & PM: Close your eyes, picture presence image, and take 3 slow, deep breaths __ Stay hydrated __ Presence activity/stress release activity __ Gratitude journal __ To sleep at bedtime	

Daily Spirit Reminders…
- Focus on the positive
- Express gratitude
- Shift your perspective on obligations as an opportunity to give

Daily Health Reminders…
- Eat real, unprocessed food
- Finish eating 3 to 4 hours before bed
- Go 12 to 14 hours between last and first meal

Daily Presentation Reminders…
- Keep up with grooming practices
- Stance check-ins

Your Future

Your Future

	Sunday	Monday	Tuesday	Wednesday	Thursday	Friday	Saturday	Reward
Week 3	__ AM, Noon, & PM: Close your eyes, picture presence image, and take 3 slow, deep breaths __ Stay hydrated __ Presence activity/stress release activity __ Gratitude journal __ To sleep at bedtime *Healthy food swap for the week: *Healthy recipe to try this week:	__ AM, Noon, & PM: Close your eyes, picture presence image, and take 3 slow, deep breaths __ Stay hydrated __ Presence activity/stress release activity __ Gratitude journal __ To sleep at bedtime	__ AM, Noon, & PM: Close your eyes, picture presence image, and take 3 slow, deep breaths __ Stay hydrated __ Presence activity/stress release activity __ Gratitude journal __ To sleep at bedtime	__ AM, Noon, & PM: Close your eyes, picture presence image, and take 3 slow, deep breaths __ Stay hydrated __ Presence activity/stress release activity __ Gratitude journal __ To sleep at bedtime	__ AM, Noon, & PM: Close your eyes, picture presence image, and take 3 slow, deep breaths __ Stay hydrated __ Presence activity/stress release activity __ Gratitude journal __ To sleep at bedtime	__ AM, Noon, & PM: Close your eyes, picture presence image, and take 3 slow, deep breaths __ Stay hydrated __ Presence activity/stress release activity __ Gratitude journal __ To sleep at bedtime	__ AM, Noon, & PM: Close your eyes, picture presence image, and take 3 slow, deep breaths __ Stay hydrated __ Presence activity/stress release activity __ Gratitude journal __ To sleep at bedtime	🎁
Week 4	__ AM, Noon, & PM: Close your eyes, picture presence image, and take 3 slow, deep breaths __ Stay hydrated __ Presence activity/stress release activity __ Gratitude journal __ To sleep at bedtime *Healthy food swap for the week: *Healthy recipe to try this week:	__ AM, Noon, & PM: Close your eyes, picture presence image, and take 3 slow, deep breaths __ Stay hydrated __ Presence activity/stress release activity __ Gratitude journal __ To sleep at bedtime	__ AM, Noon, & PM: Close your eyes, picture presence image, and take 3 slow, deep breaths __ Stay hydrated __ Presence activity/stress release activity __ Gratitude journal __ To sleep at bedtime	__ AM, Noon, & PM: Close your eyes, picture presence image, and take 3 slow, deep breaths __ Stay hydrated __ Presence activity/stress release activity __ Gratitude journal __ To sleep at bedtime	__ AM, Noon, & PM: Close your eyes, picture presence image, and take 3 slow, deep breaths __ Stay hydrated __ Presence activity/stress release activity __ Gratitude journal __ To sleep at bedtime	__ AM, Noon, & PM: Close your eyes, picture presence image, and take 3 slow, deep breaths __ Stay hydrated __ Presence activity/stress release activity __ Gratitude journal __ To sleep at bedtime	__ AM, Noon, & PM: Close your eyes, picture presence image, and take 3 slow, deep breaths __ Stay hydrated __ Presence activity/stress release activity __ Gratitude journal __ To sleep at bedtime	🎁

Daily Joy Reminders…
- Focus on the good and sprinkle joy throughout each day
- Nurture positive relationships
- Express love and appreciation

Daily Organization Reminders…
- Set aside time each day to keep organized and clean

Daily Future Reminders…
- Your future is only limited to what you can dream of and are willing to work toward
- You can make your grandest dreams come true

CONCLUSION

Your life's journey is just that, a journey, that takes time and is never going to be done until your life is over. Targeting your life and continually working to improve yourself takes hard work and effort. It's normal to have times when you feel discouraged, frustrated, or off track. When that happens, know the feelings will pass. Here are some ideas to get through funks: journal about what's bothering you and go back and see if your thoughts are really true or what you can do to fix things, list all the things you're grateful for in your life, write down all the things you've already accomplished (these can even be small steps you've taken in the direction toward a target), take a day or a week off, call a friend, go on a walk, help someone, do some extra volunteering, or go on a vacation. Don't give up on yourself!

Remember none of your targets are set in stone. As you try, experience, and learn new things you may want to change or add to your targets. Always give yourself permission to change your mind. Life is about evolving, growing, and seeing things from different and new perspectives. That will possibly change your targets, but it doesn't mean you should wait to set them. You want to always be the one purposely directing your life. The earlier you begin directing your life the better, but it's never ever too late to start. Never stop reviewing, evaluating, and resetting your targets as necessary. I recommend having a ritual of reviewing your targets, actions, and accomplishments at least yearly.

Also, remember as you go along the journey toward your targets to enjoy the now and the process. Don't wait to "be happy" once you've reached your targets. We're only guaranteed the moment we're in. Make sure to appreciate and find joy in each day along your life's journey.

ACKNOWLEDGEMENTS

I want to express my gratitude and appreciation to Jenny Merrill and David Wadsworth for their encouragement, support, advise, and help in editing this book. Thank you!

www.ingramcontent.com/pod-product-compliance
Lightning Source LLC
Chambersburg PA
CBHW050455110426
42743CB00017B/3366